T0293100

Augmenting Public Relations

Augmented Public Relations examines how existing technologies used in Public Relations (PR) are being significantly augmented because of the advent of Artificial Intelligence (AI). The book describes the opportunities and pitfalls of AI, recent and emerging technologies, and projections in their development, offering an introduction to practitioners on how they, too, can create their own AI-enhanced tools.

The developments in augmented, virtual and meta-reality, aided by AI, have now become serious contenders for commercial communication, and the ability to harness this visual capability is explained in some detail. As is the ability for practitioners to automatically monitor and feed websites using Application Programming Interfaces (APIs). The book also considers computer games as a form of communication, and the evolving application of games supported by AI. In recent years, the PR monitoring industry has deployed AI to search for content of interest to clients across a vast range of media. It throws up huge amounts of data to be managed. The book explores how such resources can be harnessed for intelligence gathering and activity deployment in easy-to-understand language. The book also covers a range of other activities from 'brain to computer communication' to chatbots, including applications used by the Internet of Things, Security Issues and Crisis Management, and the crucial subject of Ethics.

Examining a range of new practices for the PR industry, and covering both principles and applications, this book will be of great value to students, academics and practitioners alike.

David Phillips, FCIPR, Fellow of the Chartered Institute of Public Relations. Former Professor of Online Public Relations at the School of Communication and Media Studies (ESCS), Portugal. Previously Lecturer at the University of the West of England, Gloucester University and Bournemouth University. He has also worked for several decades in industry with roles including Director at Klea Global, Head of Digital at Publicasity, Corporate Affairs Director at Lancer Boss Group and Founder/Managing Director of Media Measurement Ltd.

Augmenting Public Relations

An Introduction to AI and Other Technologies for PR

David Phillips

CRC Press
Taylor & Francis Group
Boca Raton London New York

CRC Press is an imprint of the
Taylor & Francis Group, an **informa** business

First edition published 2025
by CRC Press
2385 NW Executive Center Drive, Suite 320, Boca Raton FL 33431

and by CRC Press
4 Park Square, Milton Park, Abingdon, Oxon, OX14 4RN

CRC Press is an imprint of Taylor & Francis Group, LLC

© 2025 David Phillips

ISBN: 978-1-032-83132-9 (hbk)
ISBN: 978-1-032-82658-5 (pbk)
ISBN: 978-1-003-50790-1 (ebk)

DOI: 10.1201/9781003507901

Typeset in Minion
by SPi Technologies India Pvt Ltd (Straive)

Contents

Foreword

I'VE KNOWN DAVID FOR over 25 years. THERE WAS A time now known as Web 1.0 (that is, the 1990s) when he and I were both considered experts in this new thing called the internet and were often asked to speak and write about its implications for public relations.

Web 1.0 became Web 2.0 (the social media age) and talk moved on to Web 3.0 ('the internet of things').

Many of us consolidated our knowledge and worked with what we had. Not David. His restless mind continued to look ahead, to ask deeper questions.

Having exhausted me at a conference we both attended in 2008 (intellectually and physically), I recall describing David as 'the youngest old person I know'.

We now speak positively about neurodivergence and how it can be a superpower. David is that pesky hyperactive child repeatedly asking 'why'.

This book is the product of a restless mind seeking answers to important questions about the implications of rapid technological innovation on an activity—public relations—that's often slow to change.

Is technology an opportunity for public relations? Yes. Is technology a threat to public relations? Also yes.

This book will help you grasp these opportunities and manage these threats.

Richard Bailey Hon FCIPR

Biographical Note

David Phillips FCIPR

- Fellow of the Chartered Institute of Public Relations (1968–Present): A long-standing role demonstrating expertise and leadership in public relations.

- Professor of Online Public Relations at Escola Superior de Comunicação Social (2008–2012): An academic position focussing on the intersection of public relations and digital media.

- Lecturer at University of the West of England (2014–2008) and Gloucester University (2008–2013): Teaching roles with a research focus on digitally mediated public relations and marketing.

- Director at Klea Global (2009–2013): Development of advanced news and information management and curation software, collaborating with international experts in language and AI.

- Head of Digital at Publicasity (2007–2011): Leadership in creating a team skilled in internet-aware practices within the organisation.

- Lecturer at Bournemouth University (2006–2007): Focused on teaching the online module of the PR degree.

- Founder/Managing Director of Media Measurement Ltd. (1984–2000) and Phillips & Company (1984–1999): Entrepreneurial roles in establishing a leading PR evaluation company and a public relations consultancy.

- Corporate Affairs Director at Lancer Boss Group (1979–1984): Managing public relations for a major material handling equipment manufacturer.

Authorship and Publications:

- Books such as Managing Your Reputation in Cyberspace (1999), On-line Public Relations (2001, 2008), and Evaluating Press Coverage' (1995).

- Contributions to academic journals and conferences, including articles on PR evaluation, the impact of digital media on PR and relationship management in corporate communication.

- Development of resources and papers on public relations media measurement and evaluation.

This career spans over several decades and demonstrates a profound impact on the field of public relations, especially in adapting to and leveraging digital and online mediums.

CHAPTER 1

Preface

T HIS BOOK IS ABOUT the technologies PR will need to prosper as AI eats the lunch of the communications industries.

PR is concerned with relationships, primarily the relationships organisations have with groups of people often known as stakeholders and the intermediaries that reach these groups, such as influencers and the media. So, public relations practitioners view themselves as relationship managers skilled at handling the nuances and complexities of relationships with and between people.

Indeed, there has been resistance to viewing public relations as subject to easy automation – to view it as an extension of a customer relationship management (CRM) approach. But is this a position it can hold? In this book, I suggest the whole PR sector has to change, driven by, horror of horrors, technology!

Almost all public relations interactions are already mediated by technology: by phone, by email or online, through mailing lists and online directories, forums and messaging services, and social media. But, the advent of AI has created a seismic shift in PR and its evolution.

At the turn of the century in *Online Public Relations* I wrote about Social Media as a game changer. Today, social media is commonplace in PR and a range of other communication professions. Today, dwarfing that last evolution are AI technologies that have been reborn and revolutionised.

Driven by AI all forms of PR will now have to go through another but much bigger change. AI has crept into most of the existing forms of communication and exposed other technologies as new forms of relationship

DOI: 10.1201/9781003507901-1

change and communication. It has created new such technologies and changes to existing activity, and offers further developments.

Simple things like drones bought from a high street shop have the power to send aerial video scenes from within the Albert Hall to around the world – an impossible feat five years ago.

The Los Angeles Times journalist Ken Schwencke created an algorithm that automatically generates a short article when an earthquake occurs.

Technology can automatically discover, write and deliver news about an earthquake across oceans, and in a split second.

So, PR is clearly subject to what was a distant rumble of technology and automation and now is shaking the foundations of the profession. This book explores how new and emerging technologies are invading the PR space and, at the same time, offering a much bigger and brighter future.

But what of the claim that relationships are a final frontier that's not yet been breached by AI, algorithms and automation?

Relationship management is now different.

Once upon a time, it was easy to find much of the information you wanted. Press clippings are a case in point. The author can recall a time when articles were cut out of newspapers and magazines with scissors (yes, that's right – scissors) and pasted into 'guard books'. Compare that with monitoring X (Twitter), LinkedIn, Instagram, Facebook, online news/magazines and print in researchable digital databases – and what is a 'Guard Book' anyway.

As more publications came online, search engines found more content faster and provided a hyperlink (and APIs) to the subject matter. With it came analytics and lots of searchable data and now, (AI-enhanced) search engines have been developed to provide results tailored to user interests, preferences and past searches. As machines learn more quickly than humans, this helps make searches faster and easier while delivering better accuracy.

The PR practitioner must now explore which search engines are available for different jobs. Google is but one with many capabilities. There are many others, and a comprehensive list of other search engines can be found at Wikipedia,[1] the online encyclopaedia.[2]

Search engines and other online services can dig deep into an unimaginably large information resource. The new forms of AI can also restructure these findings to help us understand this wealth of knowledge.

But is all this information too much?

To begin to practice, the PR person must access some of these data to identify stakeholders and their attitudes towards the organisation, their culture and the relationships that support their survival and success.

Now it is commonplace, but in the words of Bradley Cooper and Lady Gaga:

> ... *Are you happy in this modern world? Or do you need more? Is there something else you're searchin' for? I'm falling. In all the good times, I find myself longin' for change. And in the bad times, I fear myself. Tell me something, boy aren't you tired trying to fill that void? Or do you need more? Ain't it hard keeping it so hardcore?*

As you may expect, this book has been partly written using AI. It saved a lot of time.

Another AI computer program helped with the research. Yet another for references. The images are yet another.

I did not use ChatGPT to write the book (and every student needs to know how to write an academic essay using AI – and make it clear that they have).

The last big change in communication is accredited to Johannes Gutenberg with the invention of the printing press around 1436 AD. The evolution of communication took another big leap forward with the web and computer-mediated social media. But now we are emerging into the next mighty change.

This time it will directly and fundamentally affect those interested in radio and television, news media, marketing, computer gaming and public relations.[3]

The universities are now getting into what this means,[4] but this change needs more engagement among the communications professions.

The impact of computer systems' ability to perform tasks usually requiring human intelligence, such as deep learning and artificial intelligence, gives us new ways to develop and broadcast conversations between different parties – humans and machines.

In its communication of 25 April 2018 and 7 December 2018, the European Commission set out its vision for artificial intelligence, which supports 'ethical, secure and cutting-edge AI made in Europe'.[5] Three pillars underpin the Commission's vision: (i) increasing public and private investments in AI to boost its uptake, (ii) preparing for socio-economic changes, and (iii) ensuring an appropriate ethical and legal framework to strengthen European values.

From such ambitions, do professional communicators have a mandate to undertake such a mission?

AI-based chatbots can respond to users based on their questions and requests in natural language, while 'natural language understanding' (NLU) allows computers to interpret complex human commands and contexts. It is a branch of artificial intelligence that uses computer software to understand input in sentences using text or speech. NLU allows computers to interpret complex human commands and contexts.

Some methods of communication use Virtual Reality, Augmented Reality and the Metaverse to create immersive experiences. The business magazine *Management Today* already has a metaverse edition.[6]

Such immersive experiences can allow multiple users to interact in a shared environment. These new forms of communication, best known today as computer games, are making it easier for people worldwide to connect and share ideas faster. This is the commercial emergence of Augmented and Virtual Reality.

Then, there is the newest capability artificial and general Intelligence. And brains now interact with computers and even 'think' images and ideas into computers and, via commonly used networks, other computers online. With computers' ability to exchange such data, we have the prospect of brain-to-computers to computers-to-brain to build human telepathy and relationships worldwide.

These technologies and their applications raise huge ethical issues and demand unbreakable assurance of provenance. Monitoring activity and its provenance will be key and provide access to the ethical and efficacious management of these new activities. Blockchain will come into its own to offer such solutions.

But what is the PR professional going to do about it?

How can we prepare for BBC news to be delivered from brain to brain[7] in a metaverse ethically and with assured provenance in 2035? How can such capability be delivered ethically? It is today that we need to dare to think such things before they creep up on us.

This is the challenge communication professionals and academia now face.

This book looks at the path to such ideas. And on the way offers ways that PR can use the technologies that have already emerged. It will not only describe the nature of these new and emerging forms of communication and relationship building, but it will also provide methods for accessing them.

Without access to these developments the PR sector is doomed as we shall see.

NOTES

1 *List of search engines* (2023) *Wikipedia.* Available at: https://en.wikipedia.org/wiki/List_of_search_engines (Accessed: 07 June 2023).

2 Wikipedia develops at a rate of over two edits every second, performed by editors from all over the world. Currently, the English Wikipedia includes 6,780,424 articles and it averages 540 new articles per day. In 2023, 812,635 registered editors made at least one edit. The reach of Wikipedia is over 30 billion page views per month.

3 *Direct brain to brain communication and the future of BCIS: Rajesh Rao* (no date) *neurotechjp.* Available at: https://neurotechjp.com/blog/rao-uw/ (Accessed: 07 June 2023).

4 *Who we are + what we do + why we do it* (no date) *MIT Media Lab.* Available at: https://www.media.mit.edu/about/overview/ (Accessed: 07 June 2023).

5 *Parliament, the European Council, the council … –European parliament.* Available at: https://www.europarl.europa.eu/RegData/docs_autres_institutions/commission_europeenne/com/2018/0795/COM_COM(2018)0795_EN.pdf (Accessed: 07 June 2023).

6 Magee, K. (2022) *How we put management today into the metaverse, Management Today.* Available at: https://www.managementtoday.co.uk/put-management-today-Metaverse/indepth/article/1750641 (Accessed: 07 June 2023).

7 *Direct brain to brain communication and the future of BCIS: Rajesh Rao neurotechjp.* Available at: https://neurotechjp.com/blog/rao-uw/ (Accessed: 07 June 2023).

CHAPTER 2

Evolution

WRITING A BOOK ABOUT the evolution of artificial intelligence seems anachronistic. And so it is.

Print would seem to be out of date. What is wrong with AR with a lecturer as the star? The big problem with such solutions is that they too will soon be out of date.

The big driver of change right now is AI. It is changing all the forms of communication we have today, and its applications give us new forms of communication almost daily.

On the other hand, print has been with us for a long time, and writing is still the most common form of mechanical communication.

Wikipedia offers us this:

> The Chinese *Buddhist Diamond Sutra*, printed by woodblock on 11 May 868, is the earliest known printed book with a precise publishing date. Movable type was invented by Chinese artisan Bi Sheng in the 11th century during the Song dynasty, but it received limited use compared to woodblock printing.

There is evidence of signs being used to convey messages tens of thousands of years earlier in caves and funerary.

Print has a long and lasting history, and semiotics (signs, symbols and signification) is much older. It is the study of how meaning is created, not what it is. Fast-forward tens of thousands of years, and we continue to develop signs, symbols and signification using technologies, most recently AI.

 DOI: 10.1201/9781003507901-2

These days, the application of semiotics is diverse, and much of it is driven by evolving applications of AI.

Writing (in many forms, dimensions and languages) still and moving pictures on many materials invaded technologies at the very beginning of computing and no more so than in coding, manuals, newsprint and books.

Print allows for easy creation of an agenda for future study and research without being driven by the shifting sands of current applications.

Without being heretical there may well be a future technology driver more potent than AI, and in this book it has been possible to talk of Artificial General Intelligence, a technology as far ahead as AI was at the turn of the century. Then there is Brain-to-Brain communication as both one to one exchanges of experience and as a form of mass communication.

Dropping a first-year Public Relations (PR) student in how PR practice can realistically use virtual reality or computer games as part of best practice will be a big step, but it is not common even as a taught subject. In print, this book can offer the idea, and the rest requires the kind of creativity needed by the profession.

One of the interesting things about modern communication is how it can hop between communication genres.

A QR code printed in a press release can point to an app which can offer a wide range of facilities from books to augmented reality monitoring a corporate affairs director briefing politicians in the Central Lobby in the Palace of Westminster. It can go further and record the conversation and offer the result as minutes of the meeting. All this without a human hand in sight.

This book invites the practitioner to examine the evolution of communication that makes this possible.

The magic spell that makes such capabilities possible is AI.

AI is changing existing forms of communication, and we become aware of it as it translates a blog post into many languages or writes large parts of a press release and re-formats a photo. But it is doing much more by making past technologies into new forms of communication. Application Programming Interfaces (API) is an example and is part of the new and changing media we will use in the next few months.

Rapid change is now the norm and here is the agenda to help understanding.

CHAPTER 3

AI Creates New PR

A T THE START OF the Industrial Revolution, there was anger and violence from traditional handloom weavers who were worried that the new machinery being installed in factories would remove their livelihoods. The Luddites are variously remembered today as prototype trade unionists standing up for the little guy against the heavy machinery of capitalism or as people burying their heads in the sand rather than facing the inevitability of technological progress.

What happened next was that rather than jobs being lost, many more were created in the rapidly expanding industrial cities. They may not have been better jobs, but people chose urbanisation and the routine of industrial jobs over the uncertainty of irregular paid work in the rural economy.

The PR industry has to change. Its bread and butter business, media relations, has been cut from under.

Newspapers are competing with online advertising from tech giants such as Google, Facebook, X and Instagram as magazine advertising revenue has declined. Magazines face similar challenges and compete with content online. While some newspapers have found success online through subscription models, others have not found a sustainable way to monetise their digital content. Despite declining readership, many newspapers and magazines maintain an extensive online presence. Some publications, such as professional journals or high-quality journalistic media, have found dedicated communities and active subscription models online. National newspapers, popular magazines and independent columns are often outbid more than independent publications or quality news outlets.

DOI: 10.1201/9781003507901-3

Media companies that embrace digital strategies and look for new revenue streams are more likely to succeed. Although the print industry is shrinking, many publications are finding ways to adapt and reach their audience online. The future of our economy depends on our ability to innovate, find new revenue models and maintain the quality and value of our content.

The impact on press relations has been profound. News stories now need to be submitted to the traditional news desk and the online media, with problems of crossover between the two to boot.

If the Industrial Revolution threatened 'blue collar' jobs and imposed tough conditions on factory workers, then the technology revolution started with the microcomputer. It is now moving on fast and threatens the livelihoods of 'white collar' office workers.

But, as this book shows, the advent of Artificial Intelligence (AI) will offer a mass of new jobs, but this time, the downward pressure on incomes need not happen.

Traditional practitioners might claim that their work needs to be more contextual and more nuanced and that there are too many variables for the whole job to be automated. They point to the downsides of even automating the most straightforward tasks: the automating of media mailshots has led to ever more significant mailbox overload and frustration from journalists in receipt of what they see as this public relations spam.

In one instance, Richard Bailey tells us that a journalist who had written emotionally about the loss of her child was included in 'motherhood' mailing lists, triggering a lot of upbeat PR messages about pregnancy and maternity despite her requests to be removed from these lists, so much for nuanced practice. Clearly, greater knowledge and sensitivity should have been applied to the broad category of 'motherhood' writers. Yet when it's so cheap to send an email to a full list, why bother? It's not as if we're returning to a world where relationships were all formed face-to-face in real life.

Well, this is a broken model. We already know that technologies underpinned by AI can prevent such horrors.

We are beyond that tipping point.

Public relations has used technology for a long time.

Search (mostly Google searches, but there are others, and AI-assisted and voice searches are increasing) has changed how the world finds information and shops for products and services.

Simply put, the advent of AI has made most PR technologies much more powerful.

So, it changed public relations.

PR-for-SEO has now been renamed digital PR, but this is a misnomer because what part of public relations is not in some way digital? That meeting with a politician will have been set up digitally, as will that interview with a senior reporter. In preparation for those meetings, the briefing paper and the Q&A document will have been researched (and written?) online. Indeed, the meeting notes and minutes will probably be recorded, written and distributed by an AI-powered app.

Senior practitioners view theirs as an advisory role. It takes judgement, and this comes with experience. It relies on relationships built up over time. They are not about to be replaced by a chatbot. However, as we shall find out, they are not able to create immersive influence as powerfully as Augmented Reality, another emerging media, as it becomes more effective with the advent of AI.

SOCIAL MEDIA IS MATURE

Over recent years, a shift towards social media structural change has become apparent. Instagram is sluggish, X (Twitter) activity has dwindled to a few tweets a week for many and platforms like Facebook and Snapchat are very much in decline. A glance at these profiles might suggest they are becoming irrelevant, a sentiment increasingly shared as individuals allocate less time to social media.

Social media's initial mission of connecting individuals has largely been sidetracked. Platforms like Facebook, Instagram and X (Twitter), which once served as community hubs, have now devolved into frenetic spaces cluttered with ads and loud opinions, prompting a diaspora of users to a variety of other platforms.

A significant proportion of younger users are gravitating towards more intimate settings, such as group chats (notably in computer games), to maintain their social connections.

The internet has become pervasive in the news business.

Online news has escaped the PC and laptop and is now read on tablets, mobiles and many other screens. It is common to watch 'television' on iPlayer and similar channels, and many new 'TV' competitors are now emerging. YouTube channels are becoming increasingly popular (the BBC YouTube channel has over a million viewers). The White House Channel is a 'TV news station' in its own right. We can expect many more such news channels.

Television remains strong, but we can expect more changes in the next decade than was brought about by the explosion in digital challenges of satellite, cable and wifi that has occurred since the late 80s. Looking forward to generally available augmented and virtual reality, there will be many more TV channels opening up.

What used to be newspaper brands now bring rather good radio and TV stations, and online radio is bundled in many new ways, even in real-time, onto commercial websites and computer games.

Most people reading online news are selective about the stories they read, while print readership delves deep into content. The decline in newspaper readership is more complex than a straight substitution.

Today, news comes from many directions, with social media group chat channels being the most newsworthy of all channels, often well ahead of most other news outlets.

This is a generalisation. For some publications, a high proportion of readership is online. The *Daily Mail* had the biggest website regarding readership (the number of articles read is a different metric), with over 6.8 million people viewing Mail Online monthly (11.6 million in print) in 2024.

THE TRANSPARENT ORGANISATION

As it turns out, a lot is going on that affects corporate affairs. Of course, we start with the watchers of corporate activities. Almost anyone can view practically any company based on its online presence and the people that republish or comment on its activities.

The nature of internet transparency and porosity makes almost all corporate activity accessible to the networked digital community. In addition, such opacity is served by third-party organisations, from Corporate Watch to Safe Call.

There are videos and stories aplenty.

Developing search technologies makes organisations more vulnerable because it is easy to look for content relating to obscure subjects that are found to have a semantic relationship with an organisation. Additionally, AI can explore straws in the wind and find relationships that provide insights into reality without its express revelation from the organisation.

Much of this affects corporate brands.

An analysis of 50,000 US consumers has found that when positive brand equity and corporate reputation are combined, the effects are even more positive than the individual power of each element. There is a multiplier effect as the corporate and brand values complement each other.

It helps deliver corporate brand values to enable consumers in a networked society to cross over from consumer to corporate values missionaries and identify with or reject them. The Cambridge Forum 2012 Reputation in Age of Protest found the same, if not expressed in such terms.

The simple truth is that the practice of corporate affairs now has a role in explicating the organisation's values and ethics where the network carries its values across what once would have been stakeholders or publics but which now are networked people with common semantic interests in the organisation, which are also reflected in their values. Semantics is now part of corporate affairs where context affects meaning. It is concerned with how speakers and listeners use their knowledge of the world to interpret what is said or written yes, pure semantics!

BEING OF THE WORLD

Details of street-by-street flooding, electricity supply and emergency food stations are available to the world in the middle of hurricanes, wildfires, natural disasters and wars.

News of battles in far-off places is instantly at the disposal of the Minister of State and ordinary elector. It is possible to observe bomb craters in Ukraine battles via satellite images and from the 'comfort' of our homes.

The QuickBird satellite, launched in 2001, can monitor humanitarian crises in troubled regions such as Niger, Zimbabwe, South Ossetia, Afghanistan and Myanmar. Such a facility is becoming increasingly and publicly available with many other applications.

The citizen can see much of what was only available to the most powerful half a decade ago and comment on it, campaign with the evidence and sway the elector's mind.

For politicians, the role of social media in their future careers is patently obvious.

To imagine that a lobbyist can attempt to change the view of a politician without a profound capability to seek out the latest and best online knowledge and its context is not realistic. For the political campaigner to underrate social media is suicide. Lobbying now needs to befriend the web.

Such change, revealed in the first four years of the 21st century, is described here in breathless prose. We have to take a deep breath to take it all in.

MEDIATED

Internet technologies, in their many forms, now mediate every area of PR activity. Web-based event management software, press clipping reporting and online scanning are available (complete with an automatic Advertising Value Equivalent calculator for the truly neandertal).

We see that communications channels change and tumble in use and fashion. From every perspective, PR has to embrace an ever-changing internet.

It is not just 'Social Media' but everything the internet offers.

Where last year, one type of practice was common (e.g. talking to a journalist), next year, the conversations will need to be encrypted just to be sure that the participants are the expected actors and the conversation is not between the old-style PR and a chatbot.

Many such developments will directly affect the nature of PR, others will change the tools practitioners already use, and the indirect effects will also play their part.

In truth, this accelerating rate of change is mostly driven by AI in its many forms.

In this book, we look at the new technologies and peek further into the future.

All these changes call for a new kind of public relations and new and valuable expertise. The old PR will be superseded.

Among these words are analyses of a wide range of relevant opportunities in these new forms of PR. There is no escaping them for PR practitioners. They represent an opportunity for practitioners to become priceless contributors to organisational and national prosperity.

CHAPTER 4

The Internet Doing Things

THE INTERNET COMES OUT OF ITS BOX

The nature of online interaction has shifted towards the dynamic, where information sparks immediate action. Networked communication possesses the potential for virality, demonstrating the immense power it holds in today's digital landscape.

The once-dominant model of communication, rooted in information dissemination, has evolved over time. While few contemporary communication theorists uphold its relevance, the informational approach has historically held sway. This model, as originally formulated by Shannon and Weaver, comprised five essential elements: an information source, a transmitter, a channel (the Internet itself), a receiver and a destination. Noise, a sixth element, refers to any disruptive interference with the message.

However, the landscape has evolved, introducing a crucial seventh element: action upon arrival. The internet, in its transformative role, has blurred the boundaries between information and action. It underscores how the digital realm not only amplifies existing modes of communication but also ushers in entirely new ways of interaction and information-sharing.

Most people imagine the internet as a form of communication driven by computers in boxes. The reality, and increasingly, the internet, has now escaped the box. It provides communication designed to activate things.

 DOI: 10.1201/9781003507901-4

One such example is facilitating data transfer from the skin to the internet, such as pulse, blood pressure, number of steps taken etc. Such information can then appear on a mobile phone, computer or even in an app.

One notable illustration of this transformation is the integration of voice-activated devices like Alexa and Google Assistant. These devices seamlessly bridge the gap between digital communication and real-world outcomes. Alexa, Google Assistant and their counterparts enable a multitude of capabilities through voice commands, from searching the internet to scheduling events, adjusting device settings and accessing personalised information.

These digital assistants extend their reach to the Internet of Things (IoT), controlling smart devices such as light bulbs, thermostats and security systems. This automation empowers practitioners to streamline routines for enhanced efficiency and convenience.

Moreover, voice-activated assistants provide hands-free media playback, facilitating the enjoyment of music, podcasts and more on connected devices. They also exert control over televisions, projectors, garage doors and augmented reality features, expanding their utility in various domains.

An extensive app ecosystem further enhances the capabilities of these digital assistants. Many third-party-developed skills/apps are available. These innovations, often designed by PR practitioners, continue to evolve and find applications in diverse fields.

Notably, companies like Domino's Pizza, Nestle, Uber, Philips Hue, Fitbit and Capital One have harnessed the potential of voice-activated assistants to enhance customer experiences and operational efficiency.

The convergence of information and actionable instruction in the digital network era transcends geographical boundaries, allowing global transmission and sharing of digital assets. This paradigm shift empowers PR practitioners to wield digital tools to make things 'do things,' revolutionising traditional practices.

The fusion of command-driven communication with artificial intelligence heralds boundless possibilities. In this digital age, the internet's capacity to interact with a wide array of tools and technologies, fostering symbiotic relationships between individuals and internet-driven 'things' and environments, emerges as a transformative force.

The integration of APIs and real-time content, spanning maps, weather, calendars, IoT and more, presents a novel dimension for PR practitioners to explore. This book delves into these opportunities, offering a contemporary perspective on leveraging them to elevate the effectiveness of the PR profession.

Indeed, the internet has transcended its origins on laptops and mobile phones, ushering in a new era ripe with possibilities. Most assistive tools now require seamless integration with APIs and services to harness their full potential. This book explores these intricacies, shedding light on how PR can harness the power of these opportunities to adapt and thrive in the digital age.

APPENDIX

These are the top assistants:

Siri – Apple's intelligent personal assistant created for iOS, macOS, watchOS and tvOS devices.

Cortana – Developed by Microsoft as an intelligent personal assistant integrated with Windows 10 devices and Microsoft 365 apps.

Samsung Bixby – Virtual assistant introduced by Samsung for their Galaxy smartphones and wearables. It focuses on device interactions and controls.

IBM Watson Assistant – Advanced conversational AI platform from IBM that can understand natural language and context. Integrates across devices and channels.

Huawei HiVoice – Voice assistant tailored for Huawei smartphones that can interact in six languages and is deeply integrated into device features.

SoundHound Houndify – Independent voice AI platform that enables developers to build conversational interfaces for products, robots and automations.

Nuance Dragon Drive SDK – Tool kit from speech recognition leaders Nuance to add conversational AI capabilities like wake word detection, speech-to-text, natural language interactions and text-to-speech features.

Mycroft AI – Open-source voice assistant that can be installed on PCs and laptops with Linux and Windows as well integrated into custom hardware products.

There are also assistants designed for specific vertical domains like enterprise workflows (IPA from SAP), healthcare (Orbita Voice) and hospitality (ALICE from GoMoment) taking a more niche approach with specialised capabilities.

CHAPTER 5

Artificial Intelligence

I N THE EVER-EVOLVING LANDSCAPE of public relations and corporate affairs, one force has emerged as a catalyst of change – Artificial Intelligence (AI). Just as a seasoned researcher seeks to understand complex phenomena, we delve into the depths of AI, its current best-in-class applications in the British context and its profound implications for the fields of public relations and corporate affairs. This chapter embarks on a journey of exploration, uncovering the innovative spirit of British AI and its transformative potential.

Artificial Intelligence, or AI, is not merely a buzzword; it is a paradigm shift that transcends the boundaries of human cognition. At its core, AI seeks to replicate human-like intelligence in machines, enabling them to learn, reason and make decisions autonomously. In the realm of public relations and corporate affairs, understanding the essence of AI is paramount.

1. Machine learning: AI systems harness the power of machine learning, a subfield that empowers algorithms to identify patterns, adapt to changing circumstances and improve performance with experience.

2. Natural language processing (NLP): NLP endows AI with the ability to comprehend and generate human language, facilitating communication and understanding in corporate communications.

DOI: 10.1201/9781003507901-5

3. Computer vision: AI systems employ computer vision to interpret and extract insights from visual data, enhancing media monitoring and analysis.

4. Data-driven decision-making: AI thrives on data, utilising it to inform strategic decisions, predict trends and personalise communications.

THE BRITISH AI ECOSYSTEM

The UK stands as a vanguard in the global AI landscape, nurturing a thriving ecosystem of innovation and collaboration. British universities, research institutions and startups have played a pivotal role in advancing AI research and applications. The nation's commitment to AI is exemplified through the work of organisations like DeepMind, OpenAI and the Alan Turing Institute.

LEADING BRITISH INNOVATIONS

Britain's commitment to AI innovation is reflected in its leading research initiatives and applications:

1. DeepMind: A British AI company acquired by Google, DeepMind is renowned for its work in AI research, particularly in the realms of reinforcement learning and healthcare. Its AI algorithms have demonstrated the ability to diagnose medical conditions and enhance patient care.

2. OpenAI: Although headquartered in San Francisco, OpenAI has strong British ties, with its CEO, Sam Altman, hailing from the UK. The organisation has made significant strides in the development of natural language processing models like GPT-4, revolutionising communication and content generation.

3. Alan Turing Institute: Named after the British mathematician and codebreaker Alan Turing, this institute is dedicated to AI research and collaboration. Its work spans various domains, including finance, healthcare and social sciences, underscoring the breadth of AI's impact on society.

TRANSFORMING PUBLIC RELATIONS AND CORPORATE AFFAIRS

AI-powered Media Monitoring

AI-powered media monitoring platforms, such as Signal AI and Meltwater, have revolutionised the way organisations track and analyse media coverage. These platforms employ natural language processing to sift through vast volumes of news articles, social media posts and online content in real time. In the context of public relations and corporate affairs, this AI-driven capability offers several advantages:

1. Real-time insights: AI-powered media monitoring provides real-time insights into brand perception, industry trends and emerging issues, enabling PR professionals to respond swiftly to opportunities and crises.

2. Sentiment analysis: NLP algorithms assess sentiment, gauging the public's perception of a brand or issue, thereby guiding PR strategies.

3. Competitive analysis: AI platforms analyse competitors' media coverage, helping organisations benchmark their performance and identify opportunities for differentiation.

4. Crisis management: AI can detect emerging crises and issues early, allowing organisations to take proactive measures in crisis management.

Personalised Communication

AI-driven personalisation has reshaped how organisations engage with their audiences. British startups like Phrasee and Zephr leverage AI to create tailored content and communications, amplifying the effectiveness of public relations efforts.

1. Email marketing: Phrasee's AI-powered platform optimises email subject lines and content to maximise engagement, resulting in higher open and click-through rates.

2. Paywall optimization: Zephr employs AI to customise paywall experiences for online readers, enhancing user engagement and revenue for media organisations.

Chatbots and Virtual Assistants

British companies like Babylon Health have harnessed AI to create chat-bots and virtual assistants that enhance customer engagement. Babylon's AI-driven chatbot offers personalised health information and symptom checking, demonstrating the potential for AI to provide tailored communications in healthcare and beyond.

1. Improved customer service: AI-powered chatbots enable organisations to provide instant, round-the-clock support to customers, enhancing their experience and satisfaction.

2. Data collection: Virtual assistants can collect user data and feedback, providing valuable insights for refining public relations and corporate affairs strategies.

Crisis Prediction and Management

AI-driven predictive analytics, exemplified by companies like Darktrace, empower organisations to anticipate and mitigate cybersecurity threats. While Darktrace specialises in cybersecurity, its technology illustrates the potential of AI in predicting and managing crises across various domains.

1. Threat detection: AI systems analyse network data to identify abnormal patterns and potential security threats, aiding organisations in averting crises before they escalate.

2. Reputation management: AI can monitor social media sentiment and detect emerging reputation risks, allowing organisations to take preemptive action.

Ethical Considerations and AI Transparency

The integration of AI in public relations and corporate affairs also raises ethical considerations. AI-driven decisions must be transparent and fair, ensuring that organisations maintain trust and credibility.

1. Bias mitigation: AI systems should be rigorously tested for bias in data and decision-making processes to prevent discriminatory outcomes.

2. Ethical AI governance: Organisations should establish clear guidelines for the ethical use of AI in public relations, aligning AI practices with broader corporate values.

CONCLUSION

However, with great power comes great responsibility. Organisations must navigate the ethical considerations of AI and ensure transparency and fairness in their AI-driven decisions. The British AI ecosystem exemplifies the potential of AI to revolutionise public relations and corporate affairs, unlocking a new era of communication and engagement. In this dynamic landscape, organisations that embrace AI will wield a powerful tool for navigating the complexities of the modern communication landscape.

Artificial intelligence (AI) has emerged as a driving force that enhances various tools and platforms. It is transforming communication tools such as Application Programming Interfaces (APIs), Internet of Things (IoT), virtual reality (VR), Search Engine Optimization (SEO), QR codes and more.

APIs AND AI: EXPANDING CONNECTIVITY

Application Programming Interfaces (APIs) serve as bridges that allow different software applications to communicate with each other. AI has injected new life into APIs by enabling them to understand and process data more intelligently.

Best-in-class British Example:

Graphcore:

- Based in Bristol, Graphcore is a British AI company that has revolutionised AI hardware. Their IPU (Intelligence Processing Unit) accelerators enable AI applications to process data faster and more efficiently through APIs. This breakthrough enhances real-time communication and decision-making in AI-driven systems.

IoT AND AI: SMART CONNECTIONS

The Internet of Things (IoT) is a network of interconnected devices that exchange data seamlessly. AI plays a pivotal role in processing and interpreting the vast amount of data generated by IoT devices, making them smarter and more responsive.

Best-in-class British Example:

ARM:

- ARM, headquartered in Cambridge, is a leading provider of semiconductor IP. Their AI-powered IoT solutions enable devices to communicate intelligently. For example, AI-driven IoT devices in healthcare can monitor patients' vital signs and send alerts to healthcare providers in real time, enhancing patient care.

VR AND AI: IMMERSIVE EXPERIENCES

Virtual Reality (VR) is all about creating immersive digital experiences. AI enhances VR by creating dynamic and responsive virtual environments, personalising experiences and improving natural language processing in VR interactions.

Best-in-class British example:

Improbable:

- Improbable, a London-based tech company, is known for its SpatialOS platform. By combining AI and VR, they've created vast, realistic virtual worlds where thousands of users can interact simultaneously. This has applications in gaming, simulations and virtual training environments.

SEO AND AI: INTELLIGENT RANKINGS

- Search Engine Optimization (SEO) is crucial for online visibility. AI-powered tools and algorithms help businesses understand user intent, analyse content and optimise websites for search engines.

Best-in-class British Example:

DeepCrawl:

- DeepCrawl, headquartered in London, offers AI-driven SEO analytics. Their platform uses AI to crawl and analyse websites, identify SEO issues, and provide actionable recommendations. This streamlines the SEO process, improving website rankings and visibility.

QR CODES AND AI: SMARTER SCANNING

- Quick Response (QR) codes have become ubiquitous for accessing digital information. AI enhances QR code scanning by improving accuracy and enabling new applications, such as augmented reality experiences triggered by scanning QR codes.

Best-in-class British Example:

Blippar:

- Blippar, based in London, specialises in visual discovery using AI and AR. They have developed AI-powered QR code scanning that not only provides information but also unlocks interactive AR content. This innovative approach adds a new dimension to QR code usage.

CHATBOTS AND AI: CONVERSATIONAL INTERFACES

- AI-driven chatbots have revolutionised customer service and communication. They use natural language processing (NLP) to engage users in meaningful conversations.

Best-in-class British Example:

Cognigy:

- Cognigy, with offices in London, offers AI-powered conversational automation. Their platform enables businesses to create chatbots and virtual assistants that can handle complex conversations. This enhances customer support and engagement.

SPEECH RECOGNITION AND AI: ACCURATE TRANSCRIPTIONS

- AI has significantly improved speech recognition technology. It enables more accurate transcriptions, real-time translation, and voice-controlled interfaces.

Best-in-class British Example:

Speechmatics:

- Speechmatics, based in Cambridge, is a leader in speech recognition and transcription services. Their AI-driven platform offers real-time transcriptions for various languages and accents, making communication more accessible and efficient.

British innovation in AI has much to offer; it has not lagged behind. Companies like Graphcore, ARM, Improbable, DeepCrawl, Blippar, Cognigy and Speechmatics showcase the depth of talent and expertise in the United Kingdom. They serve as prime examples of how British ingenuity harnesses AI to propel communication tools into the future, ensuring that the world stays connected, informed and engaged in increasingly intelligent ways. As we continue to explore the synergies between AI and communication, we can anticipate even more exciting developments on the horizon.

In the meantime there are other considerations to inform the practitioner.

THE JOBS THREAT

In 2023, according to a Goldman Sachs report, over 300 million jobs worldwide could be disrupted by AI, and the global consulting firm McKinsey estimated at least 12 million Americans would change to another field of work by 2030.

The World Economic Forum estimated that 83 million jobs worldwide would be lost by 2028 because of AI, with 69 million jobs created, leaving 14 million jobs that will cease to exist. Even the people who (like PR practitioners) retain their jobs will experience a massive shift in how they do their work: The World Economic Forum says that 44% of workers' core skills are expected to change in this decade.

RATE OF CHANGE

All this is happening faster than experts predicted. In 2017, McKinsey estimated that robust large language models (LLMs) such as GPT-4 would be developed by 2027. But they are already here. And seemingly overnight, OpenAI's generative AI was integrated into Microsoft and, with a similar corpus, Google products (Google also stated that 'AI systems should be able to mine publishers' work unless companies opt out').

In a few months, corporate giants, including Amazon, AT&T, Salesforce and Cisco, rushed to incorporate enterprise-grade AI tools.

McKinsey has predicted that around 2030 and 2060, half of today's work tasks will have been automated. Their best guess as to when this will happen – 2045 – is almost a decade earlier than previously estimated.

Anu Madgavkar, a partner at the McKinsey Global Institute, predicts media jobs across the board – including those in advertising, technical writing, journalism and any role that involves content creation – may be affected by ChatGPT and similar forms of AI.

But there is a note of caution from Nobel laureate Paul Krugman, who dampens expectations over AI, like ChatGPT. He says: 'History suggests large economic effects will take longer than many people seem to expect'.

How much longer is a moot point, but there remains a certainty that change will come.

GOOD OR ILL

It is still too early to say whether AI will be used for good or evil. If past experience is anything to go by, both positions are probable (e.g. X/Twitter, which has been a boon for many and is also atrocious and dangerous for others). Knowing AI's potential risks and benefits is important to make informed decisions about developing and using this technology.

A few of the potential risks often talked about include:

- Ill-founded and ill-considered government policies and regulations. It is all too easy for such barriers to prevent all nations from being frustrated and losing the potential for a competitive edge and economic survival.

- AI has allowed the development of autonomous weapons capable of killing without human intervention. Developing the most powerful and sophisticated autonomous weapons could lead to a new, ever more deadly, arms race.

- Artificial intelligence could create a superintelligence that is more intelligent than humans. The threat of a superintelligence eliminating us poses an existential threat to humanity.

- AI could displace many jobs by automating them, leading to widespread unemployment. There could be a significant impact on the economy and society as a result of this.

- The bias of AI systems is that they are trained on human-created data. This means that AI systems can be biased, reflecting the biases in the data. Certain groups may be discriminated against as a result.

As many, if not more, experts counter such scenarios.

Here are some of the potential benefits of AI:

- Managing ethical behaviours in organisations.

- Solving problems: AI is now used to solve some of the world's most pressing problems, such as climate change and poverty. AI can be used to develop new technologies that could help us reduce our carbon emissions and improve our agricultural yields.

- Improving our lives: AI could improve our lives in many ways. AI is used to develop new medical treatments, create more efficient transportation systems and provide us with personalised education and is already offering developments in entertainment.

- Creating new jobs: AI is creating new jobs in developing, maintaining and operating AI systems. AI could also create new jobs in industries that are disrupted by AI, such as PR, manufacturing, construction and transportation.

It is important to weigh AI's potential risks and benefits before developing and using this technology (e.g. applying chatbots in education[1]).

THE TOOLS TO HELP

There are a lot of helpful AI tools that the practitioner can use. Some AI programs can identify a voice, face or other physiological traits[2] and act accordingly. If an actor says, 'turn on the TV', the sound sensors detect the voice's owner and turn it on. Many people use commands and voice recognition with Alexa and Google similarly.[3]

Interesting software (like: https://writesonic.com/, https://beta.Jasper. ai, https://chatgpt4.ai/ and https://robotalker.com/) using artificial intelligence (AI) tools can be used to automate many of the tasks involved in communication and relationship management.[4] A comprehensive list of AI tools can be found at Insidr.ai by Lasse Linnes and Matt Wolfe who run FutureTools (https://www.futuretools.io). They are among the best-informed authors, alongside Andrew Bruce Smith, in this field.

Other AI software, and there is a lot of it, such as Perplexity, which provides cited sources, Quizify creates Quizzes, FloClog offers software as a service (SAAS) for financial projections, Bearoven creates royalty-free music and highlights will summarise and take notes from YouTube videos in seconds. There is now no need to write up meeting notes or summarise conference call; AI does it for you.

The significance of AI can be seen in the rules being considered by the UK government in its 2023 White Paper.

The White Paper[5] outlines five principles that regulators should consider to facilitate the safe and innovative use of AI in the industries they monitor. The principles are:

- Safety, security and robustness: applications of AI should function in a secure, safe and robust way where risks are carefully managed

- Transparency and explainability: organisations developing and deploying AI should be able to communicate when and how it is used and explain a system's decision-making process in an appropriate level of detail that matches the risks posed by the use of AI

- Fairness: AI should be used in a way that complies with the UK's existing laws, for example, the Equality Act 2010 or UK GDPR, and must not discriminate against individuals or create unfair commercial outcomes

- Accountability and governance: measures are needed to ensure there is appropriate oversight of the way AI is being used and clear accountability for the outcomes

- Contestability and redress: people need to have clear routes to dispute harmful outcomes or decisions generated by AI.

The public relations practitioner might want to automate practices such as generating a major article. Once written, the Auto-GBT program would automate a process from beginning to end. This program would submit an article and several 'AI created pictures' to the client for approval, incorporate any corrections automatically and then work on the publishing process.

More tools are on their way. Andrew Bruce Smith has created an AI stack for practitioners:

- PR Campaign Plan Builder: https://lnkd.in/e7EghSy3

- GA4 for PR expert: https://lnkd.in/e276DaUg

- AI PR expert: https://lnkd.in/ei6WGC3W

- PR Creative Director: https://lnkd.in/es83r3FE

With more to come

Of course, the powerful Ethcs AI provided by Andrew for the CIPR is also important https://rb.gy/60glme.

However, let's be clear there are alternatives to ChatGPT. For example:

1. Chatsonic[6]

2. OpenAI playground[7]

3.   Jasper Chat[8]

4.   Bard AI[9]

5.   LaMDA (Language Model for Dialog Applications)[10]

6.   Socratic[11]

7.   Bing AI[12]

8.   DialoGPT[13]

9.   Megatron-Turing Natural Language Generation[14]

10.   Chatsonic on Opera[15]

Today, you can use AI to write music, even if you can't play a single instrument. It may not be as good yet as a professional musician, but it's much better than you could do without skills.

Already it is possible to create images from the mind with your words alone, prompts that generate fantastical images, views of worlds that have never existed or memories that encompass the best of what you remember.

Practitioners can now tell concise stories in motion pictures or write the outlines of stories and have machines draft the actual copy, the prose that fleshes out the skeleton of your idea.

And no matter how mediocre these AI-driven skills are today, tomorrow, they will be better. And the day after that, better still. AI is maturing faster than any human could, and as long as you have the skills to operate AI (mainly through prompt engineering), your access to these skills is maturing at the same rate as the machines.

Think about it for a moment. What would the world be like if your ideas could be brought to life? If others could enjoy the art that lives inside you in the way you envisioned it? How would that change the lives of the people around you? How would that change your life if you knew what was within your heart and mind could be accurately expressed?

As the British AI landscape continues to flourish, the field of public relations and corporate affairs stands at the precipice of transformation. AI-driven innovations in media monitoring, personalised communication, chatbots, crisis management and predictive analytics offer new avenues for enhancing engagement, managing reputation and achieving communication and relationship goals.

NOTES

1 https://newatlas.com/author/loz-blain 'NVidia's New Text-To-Video AI Shows an Insane Rate of Progress,' *New Atlas*, 24 Apr. 2023, newatlas.com/technology/nvidia-text-to-video-ai (Accessed: 13 June 2023).

2 Minaee, Shervin (2 July 2020) 'A survey on facial expression recognition using deep learning techniques,' *Journal of Critical Reviews*, 7(14). doi:10.31838/jcr.07.14.251.

3 Simplilearn (2023) *How does artificial intelligence (AI) work and its applications [updated], Simplilearn.com.* Available at: https://www.simplilearn.com/tutorials/artificial-intelligence-tutorial/how-does-ai-work#how_does_ai_work_and_applications_of_ai (Accessed: 07 June 2023).

4 'What Is a Chatbot? | IBM,' *www.ibm.com*, www.ibm.com/topics/chatbots#:~:text=the%20next%20step-

5 'UK unveils world leading approach to innovation in first artificial intelligence white paper to turbocharge growth,' *GOV.UK*, 29 Mar. 2023, www.gov.uk/government/news/uk-unveils-world-leading-approach-to-innovation-in-first-artificial-intelligence-white-paper-to-turbocharge-growth

6 https://writesonic.com/blog/chatgpt-alternatives/#chatsonic

7 https://writesonic.com/blog/chatgpt-alternatives/#openai-playground

8 https://writesonic.com/blog/chatgpt-alternatives/#jasper-chat

9 https://writesonic.com/blog/chatgpt-alternatives/#bard-ai

10 https://writesonic.com/blog/chatgpt-alternatives/#lamda-language-model-for-dialog-applications

11 https://writesonic.com/blog/chatgpt-alternatives/#socratic-by-google

12 https://writesonic.com/blog/chatgpt-alternatives/#microsoft-bing-ai

13 https://writesonic.com/blog/chatgpt-alternatives/#dialogpt

14 https://writesonic.com/blog/chatgpt-alternatives/#megatron-turing-natural-language-generation

15 https://writesonic.com/blog/chatgpt-alternatives/#chatsonic-on-opera

CHAPTER 6

What Is Deep Learning?

W E ARE QUITE USED to sifting through handfuls of metaphoric sand. Much of this is done using search engines or messages that come up on screens based on search criteria submitted by you. Across the metaphoric beach, there are small sand castles like SEO-optimised web pages, Twitter feeds, Facebook and Linkedin notifications blowing grains of sand across sand dunes.

In the ever-evolving landscape of artificial intelligence (AI), one paradigm has emerged as a driving force behind transformative breakthroughs: deep learning. As we navigate this era of digital communication, understanding the intricacies of deep learning and its application in the realm of public relations (PR) is essential. Here we embark on a journey to explore the profound implications of deep learning on AI and its role in reshaping communication practices in the field of PR.

Deep learning, a subset of machine learning, represents a revolutionary approach to AI that mimics the human brain's neural network. It has gained remarkable prominence in recent years, fueling advancements in diverse domains, from image and speech recognition to natural language processing and autonomous vehicles. To comprehend its significance, we must delve into its fundamental principles and grasp how it catalyzes innovation.

At the core of deep learning lies the neural network, a computational structure inspired by the human brain's interconnected neurons. These artificial neural networks consist of layers, with each layer comprising multiple interconnected nodes or artificial neurons. The depth of these networks, which can span multiple hidden layers, is where deep learning derives its name.

DOI: 10.1201/9781003507901-6

The power of deep learning resides in its ability to automatically learn and extract hierarchical features from data. This hierarchical feature representation enables the system to discern complex patterns, abstract concepts and nuances within vast datasets, a feat that traditional machine learning methods struggle to achieve.

Crucially, deep learning relies on a concept known as backpropagation, which fine-tunes the model's parameters iteratively. This process involves comparing the model's predictions with the actual outcomes and adjusting the network's weights and biases accordingly. Over successive iterations, the model refines its internal representations, enhancing its predictive accuracy.

One of the most prominent applications of deep learning is in the realm of image recognition. Convolutional Neural Networks (CNNs), a specialised architecture within deep learning, have revolutionised image classification tasks. These networks excel at identifying intricate patterns, objects and features within images. As a result, they find extensive use in facial recognition, autonomous vehicles, medical imaging and even content moderation on social media platforms.

Natural Language Processing (NLP) is another domain where deep learning has made a profound impact. Recurrent Neural Networks (RNNs) and transformer-based models, such as BERT and GPT, have transformed how machines understand and generate human language. These models have elevated machine translation, sentiment analysis, chatbots and content generation to unprecedented levels of accuracy and sophistication.

In the realm of AI-driven communication and PR, the implications of deep learning are nothing short of transformative. We witness a paradigm shift in how organisations engage with their audiences, analyse sentiment and craft personalised messages.

Sentiment analysis, for instance, benefits significantly from deep learning models' ability to comprehend nuanced language patterns. PR practitioners can employ these models to gauge public sentiment surrounding their brand or campaign. By analyzing vast amounts of social media posts, comments and reviews, AI-powered sentiment analysis tools can provide real-time insights into public perception, allowing for proactive crisis management or tailored messaging.

Personalisation in communication is another realm where deep learning shines. Recommendation systems, which leverage deep learning to analyse user behaviour and preferences, drive content curation on digital platforms. PR professionals can harness these systems to deliver tailored content and messages to their target audiences, enhancing engagement and brand loyalty.

Moreover, chatbots and virtual assistants powered by deep learning-driven NLP models offer new avenues for engaging with stakeholders. These AI-driven entities can provide instant responses to inquiries, schedule appointments and even handle routine customer service tasks. In the age of 24/7 digital communication, they serve as invaluable assets, ensuring swift and efficient interactions with the public.

Deep learning also plays a pivotal role in media monitoring and analysis. By sifting through vast amounts of news articles, blogs and social media posts, AI systems can identify emerging trends, track competitor activity and assess the impact of PR campaigns. This data-driven approach empowers PR practitioners with actionable insights to refine their strategies and messaging.

Furthermore, the emergence of AI-generated content presents intriguing possibilities for PR. Deep learning models like GPT-3 can craft coherent and contextually relevant articles, press releases and even social media posts. While human oversight remains essential, these AI-generated drafts can expedite content creation and free up PR professionals to focus on strategy and relationship building.

In the context of public relations crisis management, deep learning holds immense potential. AI-driven models can swiftly identify potential crises by monitoring online conversations and news reports. This proactive approach allows organisations to address issues in their early stages, mitigating reputational damage. Additionally, deep learning powered chatbots can provide consistent and empathetic responses during crises, ensuring timely communication with concerned stakeholders.

The integration of deep learning with augmented reality (AR) and virtual reality (VR) presents novel opportunities in PR. Immersive experiences can be tailored to engage audiences in innovative ways, offering virtual product launches, tours or interactive storytelling. Deep learning algorithms enhance the realism and interactivity of these experiences, creating memorable engagements with the public.

While the potential of deep learning in AI-driven communication and PR is undeniable, it is not without challenges. Ethical considerations, such as bias in AI algorithms and data privacy concerns, must be addressed vigilantly. Transparency in AI decision-making processes is imperative to build trust with stakeholders.

Moreover, the dynamic nature of online communication necessitates continuous adaptation. Deep learning models require ongoing training and fine-tuning to stay relevant in a rapidly evolving digital landscape. PR professionals must remain agile and vigilant in leveraging the latest advancements in AI and deep learning to their advantage.

In conclusion, deep learning stands as a cornerstone of AI-driven transformation in public relations and communication. Its ability to decipher complex data, understand language nuances and personalise interactions redefines how organisations engage with their audiences. PR practitioners who embrace deep learning and AI technologies stand to gain a competitive edge in the digital age. In this book, there is an opportunity to grasp practical ways to embrace these opportunities without having to delve too deep into deep learning. As we navigate this ever-evolving landscape, the fusion of human expertise with AI-powered insights promises to shape the future of PR and communication in unprecedented ways. The journey into the digital age continues, guided by the neural networks that emulate our own cognitive processes, and the possibilities they bring are boundless.

CHAPTER 7

Create Your Own AI

Just using ChatGPT or other fashionable AI tools is good for the elementary use of LLM (Large Language Models – see Chapter 4), but there are many other examples of AI. They have many applications, variations and capabilities that are available that are not obvious at first sight.

Artificial Intelligence (AI) allows software applications to become more accurate in predicting outcomes without being explicitly programmed. Artificial Intelligence algorithms use historical data as input to predict new output values.

In fact, AI is part of most things you do that involve electricity. AI is being used by businesses of all sizes to improve their operations and make better decisions. According to a Bard (AI) response, some everyday use cases of AI for business include:

1. AI can predict future trends, such as stakeholder sentiment, customer behaviour, product demand and financial performance. This information can be used to make better business decisions, such as PR strategy, media positioning, what products to launch, how much inventory to order and when to raise prices. It also identifies fraudulent transactions, such as credit card and insurance fraud. This can help businesses protect themselves from financial losses.

2. AI can segment stakeholders into groups based on their relationships; attitudes towards organisations, each other and competitors; demographics; inter-relationship interests; and behaviours.

 DOI: 10.1201/9781003507901-7

This information can be used to target stakeholders more effectively and improve relationships and reputation.

3. AI can identify messages and recommend media, products and services to stakeholders based on their past behaviours, opinions, purchases, views, online reactions or browsing history. This can help businesses increase margins and sales and improve customer relations.

4. In international affairs and politics, AI is a tool for examining the quality of relationships and a view into the future. In addition, it can take heed of the ethics of such publics.

These technologies can assess the risk of a particular event, such as reputation risk, a loan default or customer churn. This information can be used to make better risk and crisis management decisions, lend money, retain customers and assess friends or foes.

It is possible to set up a personal AI in ChatGPT, among others, and was explained by the leading PR commentator Neville Hobson in his blog https://rb.gy/60glme.

As AI technology continues to develop, we can expect to see even more innovative applications of this powerful technology in the future.

Most of all, these capabilities operate in the cloud, and exposing corporate data to the world's internet computers and users is a potential threat.

But how can we offer safe AI

Bearing the above considerations in mind, implementing AI is the next consideration for organisations.

We start by establishing a vision. What do you want to achieve by implementing AI? It is sensible not to create a single AI engine for all the tasks that can use AI.

Can the AI tools being used be integrated later if needed?

According to a request to AI tool Jasper, the next task is to 'Define data requirements: What data do you need to train Artificial Intelligence tools? This data should be accurate, complete, and relevant to the problem you're trying to solve'. Much of data resources will come from APIs (see below) and it will take time to find the right ones.

In setting up AI ambitions, some people and actions will be needed.

1. Establish roles and responsibilities: Who will develop, deploy, and maintain AI models?

2. Set up a change management process: How to communicate the changes AI will bring to clients?

3. Establish monitoring and revalidation: How will these outputs monitor the performance of AI tools and ensure they're still working effectively?

Implementing AI can be a complex process, but it can be a valuable investment for businesses looking to improve their operations and make better decisions.

Following these steps can increase the chances of success.

- Use AI to automate tasks: AI can automate repetitive tasks like customer service or fraud detection. This can free up employees to focus on more strategic tasks.

- Use AI to make better decisions: AI can predict future trends, identify risks and make better business decisions. This can help improve the bottom line.

- Reputation, relationship management and management of media are big opportunities for most clients. The ROI is significant.

- Use AI to improve customer experience: AI can personalise marketing campaigns, recommend products to customers, and provide better customer service (chatbots are an example). This can help attract and retain customers.

- Use AI to innovate: AI can be used to develop new products and services, improve business processes and find new ways to compete. This can help stay ahead of the competition.

AI is a powerful tool that can be used to improve businesses in various ways. Understanding how AI works and how to use it to advantage can make practitioners, consultancies and clients more efficient, profitable and competitive.

OK, so we know all that but how to implement these fine objectives?

Creating an AI engine from scratch is a huge undertaking. Most people in Public Relations (PR) will want to avoid being involved. If they do, the competencies needed are beyond the remit of this book.

But all is not lost. There are several ways AI can be implemented without being a software guru.

But why should a PR practitioner want to develop an AI tool?

Perhaps it is to interrogate relationships across social media and, as can be found at the 'List of social networking services' on Wikipedia, there are many more such sites than are normally considered by most marketers.

An AI engine can be created to monitor dozens of social media sites, blogs, podcasts, message boards, websites, news sites and many other online properties. It can track words and hashtags, names, dates, subject matter and relationships between and the strength of relationships over time. It can be designed to provide alerts and offer forward projections of users, subjects, relationships and much more all in the blink of an eye. What is more fun is that all this can be created by practitioners using an already existing wide range of AI tools.

ChatGPT4 offers this description of AI as a Service (AIaaS) in the style of Bill Bryson:

Well, folks, gather 'round as we embark on a journey into the realm of Artificial Intelligence as a Service, or AIaaS as the clever folks like to call it. Picture this: Big companies and spry start-ups have taken the plunge, offering up AI algorithms like a lavish buffet, and all you need is a ticket to the cloud'.

AIaaS, my dear readers, is like a genie in the digital lamp. It's a cloud-based marvel that opens the doors to AI capabilities for businesses without the hassle of setting up and tending to their own AI infrastructure. It's like having a gourmet meal delivered to your doorstep without the need for a fancy kitchen.

Now, the possibilities with AIaaS are as vast as the open sea. It's a versatile tool that can be summoned for a myriad of tasks. From crunching data numbers to recognizing Aunt Mabel's cat in that family photo, AIaaS has got your back.

But wait, there's more! Let's talk about the perks, shall we? First off, it's the champion of cost-effectiveness. Instead of shelling out a small fortune on building and maintaining your own AI castle, AIaaS offers a more budget-friendly way to dip your toes into the AI waters. It's like having a five-star meal without the hefty bill.

And here's the kicker: scalability. AIaaS can grow or shrink at your command, like a magical potion tailor-made for your needs. Traditional AI solutions might scoff at the idea of flexibility, but AIaaS says, 'Bring it on!'

Now, let's talk speed. Time is of the essence, my friends, and AIaaS is the hare in this race. It gets businesses up and running with AI faster than you can say 'Artificial Intelligence'. It's like the Express Lane at the supermarket but for your AI dreams.

But hold your horses, there's a cavalcade of AIaaS providers vying for your attention. Google Cloud AI, with its suite of machine learning services, is like the tech-savvy cousin who always has the latest gadgets. Microsoft Azure AI is a comprehensive AI toolkit, ready to tackle any task with its cognitive prowess. IBM Watson, AWS AI by Amazon, DataRobot, OpenAI, Clarifai, and BigML are all in the mix, each with their own bag of tricks.

Now, here's the fine print: reliability. Many of these vendors are as dependable as an old pickup truck, but there's always the chance of a hiccup or two. It's like having a reliable friend who occasionally cancels plans at the last minute. So, it's essential to do your homework and ensure your chosen AIaaS provider aligns with your expectations.

In this world of AIaaS, my friends, the keys to the kingdom are in your hands. So, choose wisely and enjoy the ride into the future of artificial intelligence, where the possibilities are as limitless as the imagination itself.

It is also possible to bring AIaaS in-house.

A few ways you could potentially bring AI as a service in-house include:

- Integrating AI-based tools or algorithms into existing software systems.
- Building an AI-powered platform or product from scratch.
- Partnering with an AIaaS provider to use their technology within your organisation.

Some key considerations for ensuring AI security in your organisation could include:

- Using encryption to protect data in transit and at rest.
- Implementing access controls to ensure that only authorised individuals can access sensitive data or systems.

- Regularly testing and updating security measures to protect against evolving threats.

- Ensuring that AI algorithms are designed with fairness, accountability and transparency.

There is also a range of big and small vendors that offer software that can be held on the client's own computer (warning AI is data-hungry) or in the cloud; some are free. Large organisations provide some such as: Google Cloud Machine Learning Engine, Azure Machine Learning Studio, H2O AI, IBM Watson, Amazon Alexa, Google Assistant and many more.

Almost inevitably, a client's AI engine will use information from one or many sites. This will include using APIs (see the chapter on APIs – the hidden media in plain sight).

Depending on how detailed a practitioner wants to go, a suitable development environment will be needed to use the chosen third-party APIs first.

Thus, using AI engines is relatively easy, and the returns are fantastic. It is a competitive advantage that cannot be missed.

There are several opportunities to be considered to bring AI as a service (AIaaS) in-house:

The incorporation of AI-powered tools or algorithms into pre-existing software systems, databases, spreadsheets in use, lists including contacts, calendars and identification of issues emerging for clients. There is more, but this is the beginning. As this book shows, there are many more areas of activity that are not immediately evident, such as applying capability to make physical things do things.

By developing a platform or product that harnesses the power of AI starting from the ground up by teaming up with an AIaaS provider, you can leverage their technology to enhance your organisation's capabilities.

When it comes to ensuring AI security in your organisation, there are several key considerations.

The utilisation of encryption is essential for safeguarding data during transmission as well as while stored securely.

One way to ensure that only authorised individuals can access sensitive data or systems is by implementing access controls.

It is imperative to continuously test and update security measures to shield against ever-changing threats.

Ensuring the design of AI algorithms incorporates fairness, accountability and transparency.

In addition, a variety of vendors, both large and small, provide software solutions that can either be installed on the client's computer (can be a data-hungry technology, so be cautious) or accessed through the cloud. A really good AI tool to use on the client's in-house data is Orange Data Mining (https://orangedatamining.com/). Furthermore, specific options are available for free. Several large organisations offer machine learning platforms, including Google Cloud Machine Learning Engine, Azure Machine Learning Studio, H2O AI, IBM Watson, Amazon Alexa, the Google Assistant and numerous other applications.

Medium-sized organizations in the United Kingdom have been increasingly turning to in-house AI software to streamline their operations and gain a competitive edge. This technological shift has been facilitated by a wave of innovative British applications that are setting new standards in the field.

ZenTech Solutions, a British tech firm, has pioneered a unique AI-driven solution called 'Mindful Management'. This in-house software is designed to enhance workplace well-being and foster a more productive work environment. It operates by analysing employee sentiment through natural language processing (NLP) and sentiment analysis. By monitoring communication channels such as emails, chat messages and even video meetings, 'Mindful Management' can identify signs of stress or dissatisfaction among employees in real time.

This innovative tool not only helps address employee burnout but also offers actionable insights to improve leadership practices. Managers can receive personalised feedback and recommendations on how to enhance team dynamics and support their staff effectively.

Procurement processes are a critical aspect of any organisation, and British application "OptiProcure" by DataSolutions UK is revolutionizing the way medium-sized companies manage their procurement operations. Leveraging advanced machine learning algorithms, OptiProcure automates and optimizes the entire procurement workflow.

This in-house AI software analyses historical data, vendor performance, market trends and even external factors like geopolitical events to make data-driven procurement decisions. It can predict when supplies need replenishing, negotiate with vendors for the best prices and even optimize inventory levels to reduce costs and minimize wastage. By doing so, OptiProcure not only saves time and resources but also enhances the strategic value of the procurement function within an organisation.

Employee training and development are crucial for the growth of any medium-sized organisation, and 'CogniCoach' by LearningAI Ltd is leading the way in personalised employee development. This in-house AI software employs adaptive learning algorithms to create customized training programs for employees.

CogniCoach assesses an employee's skills, strengths, and weaknesses through interactive assessments and ongoing performance monitoring. It then tailors training content and delivery methods to suit the individual's learning style and pace. This personalised approach not only accelerates skill development but also maximises employee engagement and retention.

Providing exceptional customer support is paramount for any organisation, and EngageTech's AI-powered solution is transforming how medium-sized businesses interact with their customers. This British application employs NLP and chatbots to enhance customer support efficiency.

Through AI-Powered Customer Support, organisations can offer 24/7 assistance, quickly resolve common inquiries and route complex issues to human agents when necessary. The AI system continually learns from customer interactions, improving its ability to provide accurate and helpful responses over time. This results in reduced response times, increased customer satisfaction and cost savings in customer support operations.

In an era of increasing cyber threats, medium-sized organisations need robust cybersecurity solutions. 'CyberGuard' by SecureNet Technologies is an in-house AI software designed to protect businesses from evolving cyber threats. This application employs advanced machine learning algorithms to detect and respond to cybersecurity incidents in real time.

CyberGuard can identify unusual patterns of network behaviour, pinpoint potential threats and take automated actions to mitigate risks. It can also adapt and evolve its threat detection capabilities as new threats emerge, making it an invaluable asset for organisations seeking to safeguard their sensitive data and digital assets.

In conclusion, British applications are at the forefront of developing in-house AI software solutions that cater to the specific needs of medium-sized organisations. These innovations, such as 'Mindful Management', 'OptiProcure', 'CogniCoach', 'AI-Powered Customer Support' and "CyberGuard," exemplify the transformative power of AI in enhancing workplace well-being, optimizing procurement processes, personalising employee development, improving customer support and strengthening cybersecurity defences. As these applications continue to evolve and adapt, they promise to drive innovation and efficiency across various sectors, benefitting organisations and their stakeholders alike.

CHAPTER 8

General Intelligence

https://www.pwc.co.uk/services/risk/insights/explainable-ai.html

The rise of artificial intelligence (AI) has catapulted the world into uncharted territory, with machines beating us at games like chess and Go and pilotless aeroplanes. But amidst this, there are two looming questions: How can I trust AI https://drive.google.com/file/d/1O_l9F-cYBNn1fVjNaW9OW_L9xVzkivOU/view?userstoinvite=%22%22 and what is Artificial General Intelligence AGI, and how does it differ from the AI we know today? Is it the Next Big Thing?

Is it a catch-all phrase to cover autonomous, self-thinking agents that will replace the human brain? It is not a single progression of AI. It is progressive and not a single development. This is one of the reasons that legislation attempting to harness the power of AI will be difficult if not impossible. The development by Google to offer enhancements to Bard is a big step towards an 'intelligent Agent' and is an example.

Open AI, the parent company of ChatGPT, marked Open AI with a mission statement in 2023:

> *Our mission is to ensure that artificial general intelligence – AI systems that are generally smarter than humans – benefits all of humanity.*
>
> *If AGI is successfully created, this technology could help us elevate humanity by increasing abundance, turbocharging the global economy, and aiding in the discovery of new scientific knowledge that changes the limits of possibility.*

DOI: 10.1201/9781003507901-8

AGI has the potential to give everyone incredible new capabilities; we can imagine a world where all of us have access to help with almost any cognitive task, providing a great force multiplier for human ingenuity and creativity.

On the other hand, AGI would also come with serious risk of misuse, drastic accidents, and societal disruption. Because the upside of AGI is so great, we do not believe it is possible or desirable for society to stop its development forever; instead, society and the developers of AGI have to figure out how to get it right.

AGI aims to emulate human cognitive abilities, including reasoning, problem-solving, understanding natural language, learning from experience and adapting to new situations. In essence, AGI strives to replicate human minds' general cognitive versatility and adaptability in machines.

Key characteristics of AGI include:

Versatility: AGI systems can perform a wide variety of tasks and adapt to new challenges without extensive reprogramming or significant changes to their underlying architecture.

Autonomy: AGI can perform tasks with a high degree of independence, making decisions and taking actions based on their understanding of the task and the available information.

Learning and Improvement: AGI can learn from experience, improving its performance over time through exposure to new data and tasks. This learning ability makes it more capable and knowledgeable over its operational lifespan.

Abstract Thinking: AGI can reason and understand concepts at an abstract level, enabling it to solve problems that require creative and critical thinking.

Natural Language Understanding: AGI can comprehend and generate human language, enabling effective communication and interaction with humans.

Transfer Learning: AGI can apply knowledge gained from one task to improve its performance on related tasks, a concept known as transfer learning.

Anticipated applications of AGI cover a vast array of domains due to its general-purpose capabilities. Some potential applications include:

Research and discovery: AGI will analyse vast data to offer comprehensive stratagems for developing organisational relationships and subsequential growth.

AGI could accelerate scientific research by autonomously analysing vast data, proposing hypotheses and designing experiments.

In medical diagnosis and treatment: AGI could aid medical professionals in diagnosing diseases, suggesting treatment plans, and even predicting potential health risks for individuals (even driving more advanced robot surgery).

AGI will revolutionise education by personalising learning experiences for students, adapting to their individual needs and providing tailored content and feedback.

AGI will (already is) power autonomous systems to, for example, automate self-driving cars, drones and robots capable of performing complex tasks in various environments.

AGI assists in creative endeavours such as writing, art, music composition and film production, potentially contributing to new forms of artistic expression.

Economic and financial analysis of economic trends, prediction of market behaviours and optimising financial strategies for businesses and individuals.

Natural language interaction and chatbots in very advanced form will use AGI systems, including advanced virtual assistants capable of understanding and responding to human language and physical movements. This will lead to improved customer support, language translation and more.

AGI simulates complex systems in scientific modeling and simulation, aiding in climate modelling, materials science and other fields requiring intricate simulations.

Problem-solving: AGI is already tackling complex problems in logistics, activity optimisation and resource allocation across industries.

Ethical and social action and implications will contribute to solving complex societal challenges by analysing various factors and proposing potential solutions.

It's important to note that AGI raises significant ethical, safety and societal concerns. Developing AGI requires careful consideration of these implications to ensure its responsible and beneficial deployment.

However, there are also some potential risks associated with autonomous agents. These agents will be used to automate/change jobs currently done by humans, leading to job reassignment. They could also be used to harm people or property and need to be properly designed and controlled.

It is essential to start thinking about how we can prepare for the rise of autonomous agents. Public relations (PR) practitioners need to develop ethical guidelines for developing and using these agents. We also need to invest in education and training so that people can develop the skills they need to work alongside autonomous agents.

The AI revolution is already here, and autonomous agents are one of the most critical technologies that drive this revolution. By preparing for the rise of autonomous agents, we can ensure that this technology is used for good and benefits all of us.

Here are some things PR can do to prepare for the rise of autonomous agents:

- Develop ethical guidelines for the development and use of AI and autonomous agents.

- Invest in education and training so that people can develop the skills they need to work alongside autonomous agents.

- Promote professional and public awareness of autonomous agents' potential benefits and risks.

The rise of autonomous agents is a complex and challenging issue. However, by preparing for this revolution, we can ensure that it is used for good and benefits all of us.

These technologies are emerging even now, and their development will accelerate.

This is yet to be key to PR practice but is an area that needs to be watched closely.

As consultants, staying informed about AGI can help us think better about the consequences of such a development and help our clients align their business strategies with the potential benefits of AGI.

The issue we face is that the role of relationship management may be an ability to manage not just human and institutional relationships but relationships with AI manifestations, which will often be intertwined with human/computer interaction.

This, then, is an area of research for PR practice if only to keep our finger on the pulse, ready to take advantage of the emerging opportunities.

Several organisations will introduce AGI services after Microsoft introduced its advanced capability in 2023 called KOSMOS-2 and Google implemented new protection against attacks using Chrome.

See below for additional background:

1. *Accountability and Transparency.* https://doi.org/10.1145/3593013.3594067

2. Hazem Zohny, J. McMillan, & M. King. (2023). Ethics of generative AI. In *Journal of Medical Ethics* (Vol. 49, pp. 79–80). https://doi.org/10.1136/jme-2023-108909

3. E. Brynjolfsson, Danielle Li, & Lindsey Raymond. (2023). Generative AI at Work. In *SSRN Electronic Journal.* https://doi.org/10.3386/w31161

CHAPTER 9

Explainable AI (XAI)

A S WE ARE INCREASINGLY governed by algorithms, AI has become an indispensable tool, shaping decisions and outcomes in fields ranging from defence to healthcare. Yet, despite its pervasiveness, AI often operates as a black box, its inner workings shrouded in mystery. This lack of transparency breeds distrust and hinders our ability to harness the power of AI fully.

The PR practitioner has to keep abreast of the relationships, reputation and ethical issues that surround the use of AI. It has to use Explainable AI (XAI).

It is a burgeoning field dedicated to illuminating the decision-making processes of AI systems. XAI seeks to bridge the gap between the intricate calculations of machines and the comprehension of humans, transforming AI from an opaque oracle into a transparent and accountable partner.

Explainable Artificial Intelligence (XAI) has become increasingly important as AI systems are deployed in more critical domains like PR, IoT and criminal justice. There is a need to make these AI systems more transparent and explainable.

Major tech companies like Google, Microsoft, IBM and Facebook have active research programs in XAI and have released XAI tools and techniques. For example, IBM's AI Explainability 360 toolkit, Microsoft's InterpretML and Google's Explainable AI. X (Twitter) has a system in place called Grok.

A twofold imperative drives the quest for explainable AI: trust and improvement. Firstly, trust is the bedrock of any meaningful relationship,

DOI: 10.1201/9781003507901-9

whether between humans or between humans and machines. When we understand the reasoning behind an AI system's decisions, we are more likely to trust its judgement and accept its outcomes. This trust is particularly crucial in high-stakes domains such as corporate PR practice, medical diagnosis or autonomous vehicles, where errors can have grave consequences.

Secondly, XAI holds the key to improving AI performance. By scrutinising the decision-making processes of AI models, we can identify biases, errors and inefficiencies.

In the realm of AI, the black-box nature of many algorithms has often been a cause for concern. However, the emergence of XAI has provided a solution to this opacity, promising greater transparency and understanding of AI systems. In this article, we will delve into the concept of XAI, its significance in AI applications and explore current best-in-class British examples that employ this cutting-edge technology.

XAI represents a critical shift in the development and application of AI systems. Traditionally, AI algorithms, particularly those based on deep learning, have been characterised as black boxes. They process data and generate predictions or decisions, but understanding how they arrive at those conclusions has often been elusive.

XAI seeks to address this issue by making AI systems more transparent and interpretable. At its core, XAI aims to provide explanations for AI-driven outcomes that can be understood by humans, including domain experts, policymakers and end-users. This transparency not only builds trust in AI systems but also enables better decision-making and accountability.

Key Principles of XAI

To appreciate the significance of XAI, it is essential to grasp its key principles:

1. Transparency: XAI systems strive to make the inner workings of AI models comprehensible. This involves providing insights into the data, features and processes that contribute to AI predictions.

2. Accountability: XAI enhances accountability by allowing users to trace the logic and reasoning behind AI-generated outputs. This is crucial, particularly in fields like healthcare, finance and law, where decisions have far-reaching consequences.

3. Fairness and Bias Mitigation: XAI can help identify and rectify biases in AI models, ensuring that they do not discriminate against particular groups or produce unfair outcomes.

4. Trustworthiness: By providing transparent explanations, XAI builds trust among users and stakeholders, making AI systems more readily adopted and accepted.

BEST-IN-CLASS BRITISH APPLICATIONS OF XAI

Now that we have a solid understanding of XAI, let's explore some exemplary British applications that incorporate XAI principles:

1. Healthcare Diagnostics: British companies like BenevolentAI[1] are leveraging XAI to enhance the drug discovery process. By providing clear explanations for the potential efficacy of various compounds, XAI accelerates the identification of promising candidates for drug development.

2. Financial Services: XAI is making waves in the financial sector, where companies like Exberry[2] are using it to improve algorithmic trading. These systems offer transparent insights into trade execution decisions, ensuring fairness and reducing the risk of market manipulation.

3. Legal AI: British legal technology companies such as Eigen Technologies[3] are applying XAI to contract analysis and due diligence processes. XAI helps legal professionals interpret complex legal documents by highlighting key clauses and potential risks.

4. Energy Efficiency: XAI is aiding the drive for sustainability in the UK's energy sector. Companies like Upside Energy[4] employ XAI to optimise energy consumption in buildings, thereby reducing costs and environmental impact.

CHALLENGES AND FUTURE DIRECTIONS

While XAI holds great promise, it is not without challenges. Developing XAI systems that are both accurate and interpretable remains a complex task. Striking the right balance between transparency and complexity is an ongoing challenge for researchers and developers. Moreover, the regulatory landscape for XAI is evolving, with a need for clear guidelines to ensure ethical and responsible AI applications.

Looking ahead, the integration of XAI into various sectors is expected to grow, driven by a combination of technological advancements and regulatory pressures. British companies are well-positioned to lead in this space thanks to their innovation and commitment to ethical AI development.

In conclusion, XAI represents a transformative development in the world of AI. Its principles of transparency, accountability, fairness and trustworthiness are reshaping the landscape of AI applications in the UK and beyond. Through best-in-class British examples across healthcare, finance, legal and energy sectors, we can see how XAI is being harnessed to improve decision-making, enhance fairness and promote responsible AI development. As the field of XAI continues to evolve, it holds the potential to revolutionise industries and improve the lives of individuals, making it a critical focus for academia and industry alike.

NOTES

1. BenevolentAI. (n.d.). https://www.benevolent.com/
2. Exberry. (n.d.). https://exberry.io/
3. Eigen Technologies. (n.d.). https://www.eigentech.com/
4. Upside Energy. (n.d.). https://upsideenergy.co.uk/

CHAPTER 10

Augmented Reality

Augmented Reality (AR) is a technology that enhances the real world by overlaying digital information, objects or experiences onto our physical surroundings. It operates on a set of core principles that resonates with the fundamentals of collaboration and learning:

> AR systems respond and adapt to real-world stimuli and user interactions, promoting immediate feedback and iterative learning.

Just as individuals in a team must recognise each other's strengths and contributions, AR applications employ computer vision to recognise and track physical objects or scenes.

AR overlays digital elements, such as 3D models, text or animations, onto the user's view of the physical world, enhancing the understanding of complex information.

Successful AR harmoniously integrates the digital and physical, fostering context and coherence, much like effective collaboration within teams.

Britain has a rich history of innovation and technological advancement. Today, it continues to be a hub for cutting-edge developments in augmented reality. Some of the most notable British AR applications have made significant strides in various domains, showcasing the country's prowess in this dynamic field.

The Royal Museums Greenwich has embraced AR technology to enhance the museum experience. Visitors can now use their smartphones

DOI: 10.1201/9781003507901-10

to access an AR guide that overlays historical ship models with digital reconstructions, providing a deeper understanding of maritime history. This application exemplifies how AR can be a valuable tool for education and engagement.

The Tate, a renowned art institution, has ventured into the realm of augmented reality with a virtual art gallery. Visitors can use AR headsets to explore curated exhibitions in an immersive digital environment. This innovation demonstrates how AR can transform the way art is experienced and interpreted, offering a novel approach to cultural engagement.

In the automotive industry, Jaguar Land Rover has introduced AR user manuals. Owners can use a smartphone app to scan different parts of their vehicles, and the app provides interactive guides and explanations. This application showcases how AR can simplify complex information dissemination, aiding in user education and enhancing customer satisfaction.

In the realm of public relations, stakeholder engagement is paramount. Organisations must effectively communicate their values, goals and initiatives to build trust and credibility. Augmented reality offers a unique avenue for engaging stakeholders, enabling companies to deliver immersive and memorable experiences.

Traditionally, annual reports are static documents that provide financial and operational summaries. With AR, organisations can transform these reports into interactive experiences. Stakeholders can scan printed reports or documents with a smartphone app, unlocking multimedia content, such as video messages from the CEO, dynamic charts and augmented reality storytelling that bring the company's achievements to life. This approach fosters deeper engagement and facilitates a collaborative learning experience for stakeholders.

Companies can use AR to create virtual corporate tours. Stakeholders, including investors, employees and the media, can explore company facilities, production processes and innovation centres from the comfort of their own devices. By providing an immersive behind-the-scenes look, organisations can enhance transparency and collaboration with their stakeholders.

Learning is a continuous process within organisations, and collaboration is the cornerstone of progress. Augmented reality can be a powerful tool for facilitating learning and collaboration in the context of corporate affairs.

When new employees join an organisation, the onboarding process plays a crucial role in their integration. AR can be used to create interactive onboarding experiences. New hires can use AR apps to access immersive training modules, learn about company history and virtually meet key team members. This approach not only accelerates the learning curve but also fosters collaboration by introducing newcomers to the corporate culture.

Developing your own AR capability may sound daunting, but with the right approach, it can be an exciting and rewarding endeavour. Here is a step-by-step guide to help you get started:

1. Define your purpose:
   Before diving into AR development, determine your specific goals. Are you looking to create a gaming application, enhance education or improve navigation?

   Clear objectives will guide your project. What are the objectives of the prospective AR experience (e.g. informing, relationship management, entertainment, marketing, learning)?

2. Choose a development platform:
   AR development typically relies on platforms and tools like Unity3D, ARKit (for iOS), ARCore (for Android), or web-based frameworks like A-Frame. Select a platform that aligns with your project's goals and target audience.

3. Acquire the necessary skills:
   Developing AR applications requires expertise in programming languages like C# or JavaScript, as well as 3D modelling and design skills. Invest time in acquiring these skills or consider collaborating with experts.

4. Gather resources:
   Collect the necessary hardware and software tools, such as AR-compatible smartphones or headsets, a computer with sufficient processing power and development software (including the

media you choose such as a kiosk, screen, smartphone, glasses, headsets, interaction to be offered (e.g. tap, swipe, voice commands, sensor).

5. Will the projection be still animated or interactive?

6. Start small:
   Begin with a simple AR project to familiarise yourself with the chosen platform. Practice is crucial in mastering AR development.

7. Design user interfaces:
   Create intuitive user interfaces (UI) that seamlessly blend digital elements with the real world. Ensure that the AR content enhances the user's experience.

8. Develop content:
   Generate 3D models, animations or interactive elements that will be overlaid onto the real world. Optimise these assets for performance.

9. Test and iterate
   Regularly test your AR application and gather feedback

10. Develop content:
    Generate 3D models, animations or interactive elements that will be overlaid onto the real world. Optimise these assets for performance.

11. Consider AR cloud: To enable persistent AR experiences, explore AR Cloud solutions that allow your digital content to be anchored to specific locations in the real world

12. Publish and share:
    Once your AR application is polished and user-friendly, publish it on app stores or platforms of your choice. Share your creation with the world!

Now that we have a basic understanding of how to create your own AR capability, we need to explore some remarkable British applications that have excelled in this field:

1. **Blippar**:
   Blippar is an AR pioneer that has made waves in the marketing and advertising sectors. Their platform allows brands to create engaging AR experiences for consumers. By scanning a product or image, users can access interactive content, such as product information, games or exclusive offers.

2. **Zappar**:
   Zappar specialises in creating AR experiences for both consumer and enterprise applications. Their ZapWorks platform empowers developers to craft immersive AR content for marketing campaigns, education and training. Zappar has partnered with renowned brands like Coca-Cola and Warner Bros. to bring AR to the masses.

3. **Immerse**:
   Immerse is a British company at the forefront of AR in the enterprise sector. They provide immersive training solutions using AR and VR technologies. By incorporating AR into training modules, Immerse helps organisations enhance learning experiences and improve employee performance.

4. **Groove Jones**:
   Groove Jones is an agency that combines creativity and technology to deliver outstanding AR experiences. They have worked on projects for major brands like Amazon, Toyota and Universal Pictures. Groove Jones showcases how AR can elevate marketing campaigns and entertainment experiences.

5. **MoorMe**:
   MoorMe is a British startup that offers an innovative AR navigation app for hikers and outdoor enthusiasts. Users can scan landmarks, and the app provides real-time information about the surroundings, trails, and points of interest. It's a prime example of how AR can enhance outdoor adventures.

CONCLUSION

As we conclude our exploration of creating your own augmented reality capability and British excellence in this field, it's evident that AR technology holds immense potential for transforming various industries. With determination, the right resources and a clear vision, you can embark on your AR development journey. The British examples mentioned here demonstrate the versatility and creativity that AR technology brings to marketing, training, navigation and entertainment. So, whether you're a budding developer or an entrepreneur, the world of augmented reality offers a playground of possibilities waiting to be explored and harnessed for the benefit of society.

CHAPTER 11

Virtual Reality

MOST RECOGNISE VIRTUAL REALITY (VR) as computer games played with a headset and handheld controllers. We will cover Games in a later chapter.

But VR goes much further than that.

This immersive environment allows users to interact with the virtual world, not just watch it. It uses computer graphics and sound to create an environment where users can move around in three dimensions.

The interactive nature of these near-real environments includes all forms of communication, from touch to images and sounds and thus provides a dopaminergic surge in the user's brain. When well done, it is the most powerful form of communication available.

The user wearing a headset is presented with a three-dimensional image generated by a computer. This is unlike standard two-dimensional (2D) images that we are used to seeing on our television sets (headsets are changing fast, and new ones look like a pair of glasses or are projectors embedded in glasses).

One of the instances that practitioners may find enlightening is this *Guardian* case study:

> The Guardian *has been a pioneer in the use of virtual reality (VR) for news reporting. In 2016, the newspaper partnered with Google Cardboard to produce a VR experience of the Syrian refugee crisis. The experience, called 'The Unquiet Frontier', allowed users to walk through a refugee camp in Jordan and hear from the people who live there.*

DOI: 10.1201/9781003507901-11

The Guardian *has also used VR to report on other major news events, such as the 2017 Manchester Arena bombing and the 2018 Grenfell Tower fire. In each case, the newspaper has used VR to give users a more immersive and emotionally engaging experience of the events.*

The Guardian's *use of VR has been praised by critics and journalists. In a review of 'The Unquiet Frontier', the* New York Times *called it 'a powerful and immersive experience' that 'brings the Syrian refugee crisis to life in a way that traditional news reporting cannot'.*

Despite the challenges, the *Guardian*'s use of VR shows that it is a promising new tool for news reporting and communication that PR practitioners can use to deliver content to a wide range of media. VR can make the news more immersive, engaging and informative.

Are you looking to create a Virtual Reality (VR) experience for your stakeholders?

Whether you're looking to build an immersive virtual tour of your office, factory, food preparation production line or something wildly different, VR is ready and waiting.

VR has emerged as a transformative technology that extends far beyond the realm of gaming. In recent years, its application in various non-gaming sectors has gained substantial traction, revolutionising industries from healthcare and education to architecture and engineering. This chapter will explore the diverse applications of VR in non-gaming contexts and highlight some best-in-class British examples that demonstrate innovation and excellence in this field.

VR has long been associated with the computer games industry, but its potential extends far beyond entertainment. As technology continues to advance, VR is finding applications in various fields, from healthcare and education to marketing and training. In this essay, we will explore how a public relations (PR) practitioner can play a pivotal role in developing and promoting VR for non-gaming applications in the UK market, with a focus on medium-sized British companies.

To effectively develop and promote VR for non-gaming applications, PR practitioners may want to understand the immense potential that VR holds across industries. VR offers a unique immersive experience that can revolutionise how businesses engage with their audiences, solve complex problems and enhance various processes. By recognising this potential, PR professionals can identify opportunities to leverage VR in innovative ways.

Building strong industry connections is crucial for a PR practitioner looking to develop VR applications for non-gaming purposes. Collaborating with experts, technology developers and industry leaders can provide valuable insights and resources needed for successful VR projects. Networking and partnerships play a vital role in staying updated on the latest VR trends and developments.

One of the primary roles of PR is to effectively communicate the value proposition of VR applications to potential stakeholders and customers. PR practitioners need to develop compelling narratives that highlight the benefits in areas such as healthcare, education, marketing and training. These narratives should focus on how VR can improve efficiency, enhance user experiences and drive positive outcomes.

Creating captivating content is essential in the world of PR. For VR applications, storytelling takes on a whole new dimension. PR practitioners should collaborate with content creators and VR developers to craft immersive and engaging experiences that resonate with target audiences. This includes creating 360-degree videos, VR simulations and interactive content that can showcase the capabilities of VR in non-gaming contexts.

PR practitioners can harness the power of media and influencers to generate awareness and excitement. Case studies and success stories from medium-sized British companies can be particularly effective in this regard.

Medical Realities, a medium-sized British company, has developed VR solutions for medical training. They offer immersive surgical training experiences for medical professionals and students. Through partnerships with medical institutions, they have successfully used VR to simulate complex surgeries, allowing trainees to practice in a risk-free environment. PR efforts have been instrumental in communicating the value of these training modules to medical schools, hospitals and healthcare professionals.

MEL Science, another British company, focuses on revolutionising science education with VR. They provide immersive chemistry experiments for students, enabling them to conduct experiments in a virtual laboratory. PR strategies have included collaborations with educational institutions, showcasing how VR enhances students' understanding of complex scientific concepts and practical skills.

Zappar, a medium-sized British company specialising in AR and VR marketing, has developed innovative solutions for brands and marketers. PR practitioners at Zappar have successfully promoted the use of AR and VR for engaging marketing campaigns. By creating interactive and immersive experiences, brands can capture the attention of their target audiences. PR has played a pivotal role in showcasing how Zappar's solutions drive customer engagement and brand loyalty.

Immerse, a British VR company, focuses on corporate training solutions. Their VR platform allows businesses to create immersive training experiences for employees, covering a wide range of industries, from manufacturing to finance. PR efforts have highlighted the cost-effectiveness, scalability and effectiveness of VR training, making it an attractive option for medium-sized companies seeking to upskill their workforce.

As VR technology continues to evolve, PR practitioners have a unique opportunity to shape its applications in non-gaming contexts. By understanding the potential of VR, building industry connections and effectively communicating its value proposition, PR professionals can play a vital role in promoting VR solutions developed by medium-sized British companies. The examples of Medical Realities, MEL Science, Zappar and Immerse illustrate how these companies have successfully leveraged VR in healthcare, education, marketing and corporate training, thanks in part to strategic PR efforts. As VR continues to expand its reach across industries, PR practitioners will remain essential in driving its adoption and success.

One of the most prominent non-gaming applications of VR is in education and training. VR offers immersive learning experiences that enhance comprehension and retention. British institutions have been at the forefront of integrating VR into education. The University of Oxford, for instance, utilises VR to recreate historical events, allowing students to step into ancient battlefields or historical landmarks virtually. This immersive approach fosters a deeper understanding of history and culture.

In the healthcare sector, VR has proven invaluable for both patients and medical professionals. Medical Realities, a UK-based company, has pioneered the use of VR in surgical training. Their platform enables aspiring surgeons to practice procedures in a realistic virtual environment, reducing the risks associated with real-life surgeries. For patients, companies like Psious offer VR therapy for mental health issues, providing an immersive and effective way to treat conditions such as anxiety and phobias.

VR has revolutionised the architecture and design industries. British architectural firms like Zaha Hadid Architects use VR to create virtual walkthroughs of their designs. This allows clients to explore and visualise architectural concepts before construction begins. Such applications not only save time and resources but also enhance client satisfaction.

In engineering and manufacturing, VR has proven to be a game-changer. BAE Systems, a British multinational defence, security and aerospace company, employs VR for designing and prototyping complex military equipment. This technology streamlines the development process and improves collaboration among engineering teams.

VR has the potential to transform the tourism industry by offering virtual travel experiences. VisitBritain, the national tourism agency, has collaborated with tech companies to create immersive VR tours of iconic British destinations. These virtual tours allow potential tourists to explore the UK's attractions, leading to increased interest and bookings.

Incorporating VR into employee training and development has become a strategic advantage for many British companies. BP, a leading energy company, utilises VR to train its employees in safety procedures and emergency response. This approach ensures that employees are well-prepared for real-world challenges, reducing accidents and incidents.

VR has opened up new possibilities in the art and cultural sectors. The British Museum has embraced VR to offer virtual exhibitions and tours of its vast collection. This allows art enthusiasts from around the world to explore the museum's treasures without leaving their homes.

In the aerospace and aviation industry, VR has become an indispensable tool for training pilots and aircraft maintenance personnel. British Airways, for instance, employs VR simulations to train its pilots in various scenarios, enhancing their skills and safety.

VR has transcended its gaming origins to become a disruptive force in numerous non-gaming sectors. British innovators and institutions have played a pivotal role in harnessing the potential of VR, exemplifying excellence in education, healthcare, architecture, engineering, tourism, training, art and aerospace. As the technology continues to evolve, the applications of VR in non-gaming contexts are bound to expand further, reshaping industries and offering new possibilities for immersive experiences and improved efficiency.

How does a PR professional create and promote a VR case study that captivates stakeholders and leaves a lasting impression? As an example, we examine how a practitioner might use VR to create a case study in VR:

Beginning by clarifying the objectives of the VR case study is pretty obvious. What message or story is to be conveyed and who is the target audience with explicate goals will guide the entire process, from content creation to promotion.

Crafting a compelling narrative is at the core of any successful case study. In VR, the narrative takes centre stage as it immerses the audience in a virtual world. The story should resonate with the audience and align with the organisation's values and mission. It could be a success story, a behind-the-scenes glimpse or an exploration of a product or service's impact.

VR content creation requires specialised expertise. Collaborate with VR developers, designers and storytellers who can bring your vision to life. Ensure that the VR experience is seamless, user-friendly and visually appealing

The process will need a script that outlines the narrative and interacts within the VR experience. Storyboarding helps visualise the scenes and transitions, ensuring that the story flows smoothly in the virtual environment.

Technically a 360-degree camera will be useful to create content. Three-dimensional modelling or computer generated images capture or create immersive content. Whether it's a virtual tour, a simulation or an interactive experience, the content should align with the narrative and engage the audience. It is worth examining the opportunity offered by AI in creating and animating images in the VR environment.

Before launching your VR case study, conduct thorough testing to identify and address any technical glitches or user experience issues. Iterate and refine the VR experience based on user feedback to enhance its impact.

Then comes the critical phase of promoting your VR case study:

The creation and promotion of a VR case study demands a strategic blend of storytelling, technology and audience engagement. By meticulously planning your VR journey, collaborating with experts and leveraging various promotional channels, you can transport your stakeholders into a virtual world that not only conveys your message but also fosters a deep and lasting connection with your brand or organisation. VR has the power to transcend boundaries and create immersive experiences that resonate with audiences in ways traditional media cannot. Embracing this transformative tool lets your PR efforts soar to new heights in the digital age.

CHAPTER 12

The Metaverse

SUPPOSE YOU WANTED TO get people from Teesside into the new exhibition in the National Gallery in London and, at the same time, get Americans from the Bronx to join in. That's a tough Public Relations (PR) call, if there ever was one.

But today, it's possible.

You simply put the National Gallery into the metaverse. In fact, as a means of taking the many icons of British culture across dying high streets into Small Town America and schools across the UK, this is the way to do it. The Arts Council could be a net taxpayer instead of a recipient of government money! Its members can become providers and distributors of the content in towns worldwide – a great way of revealing the British national culture to the world.

The metaverse allows people and things, as well as virtual objects, to interact with each other in new and exciting ways.

Although Facebook CEO Mark Zuckerberg may be credited with popularising the term 'metaverse', it wasn't his idea in the first place. Tech firms have been focussing on this for a long time.

The metaverse is an expansive network of persistent, real-time rendered 3D worlds and simulations that support continuity of identity, objects, history, payments and entitlements, and can be experienced synchronously by an effectively unlimited number of users, each with an individual sense of presence,

wrote venture capitalist Mathew Ball.

DOI: 10.1201/9781003507901-12

The progressive evolution and interactive capability allow users and software to communicate with facial and physical movements. The emerging technology comprises a network of virtual platforms, applications and capabilities that enables users and the metaverse environment to create new content, experiences and interactions (see also Chapter 20). In its most basic form, a metaverse has a sense of immersion, real-time interactivity, user agency and persistence (imagine getting up close to see the brush strokes of Claude Monet's *Bathers at La Grenouillère* with your artist boyfriend in a once empty high street shop nearby in Teesside).

The metaverse, which is a virtual shared universe where people can engage in social, economic, and cultural activities using immersive technologies such as augmented reality (AR) and virtual reality (VR), also developed from the convergence of various existing technologies and external factors. A complex interplay of various social factors influenced the rapid emergence of metaverse technology and services. The pandemic shifted interpersonal communication in a face-to-face environment to online-centered communication. As distanced and virtual activities and physical distancing became more common, people had to rely on digital media platforms and technologies for their everyday social interactions. Along with existing social media platforms like Facebook, Twitter, and Instagram, people began to seek new formats of social media, including metaverse-originated applications such as Zepeto.[1] Technological advances were another major factor in the development of the metaverse. Information and communication technology innovations (such as AR, VR, and 5G networks) have been fused to create an environment where the metaverse can be implemented. The 'digital native' generation easily accepts such technology, creating avatars and communicating with others in the virtual world.[2] (ISSN 0040-1625, https://doi.org/10.1016/j.techfore.2023.122980) (https://www.sciencedirect.com/science/article/pii/S0040162523006650) Technological Forecasting and Social Change, Volume 198, 2024

The Economist YouTube video, 'How will businesses use the metaverse?' is also an excellent introduction to the business of the metaverse. An immersive virtual press conference is now a practical opportunity with a computer moderating, creating and enhancing journalists' questions.

More interesting will be taking learning into the classroom and allowing employees to explore virtual reality simulations of their classroom and work environments.

Metaverse technology gives users the potential to create meaningful, interactive experiences across a variety of platforms, from digital art galleries and computer game worlds to virtual conferences and educational courses, all made possible through advanced graphics and artificial intelligence (AI). For example, one application could be a metaverse-powered virtual shopping experience.

Of course, a wide range of organisations are already using metaverse. To run metaverse events (including press conferences) is easy. Some companies already have a 'platform' on which the practitioner can impose the environment they wish to create.

The audience size and uptake of this new medium are quite significant.[3]

- The projected value in the Metaverse Live Entertainment market for the United Kingdom reached £7.8m in 2023.

- Regarding user numbers, the Metaverse Live Entertainment market in the United Kingdom is expected to have approximately 30.1k users by 2030.

- The United Kingdom is experiencing a surge in demand for immersive live entertainment experiences within the metaverse.

United Arab Emirates' Ministry of Economy has its own headquarters in a metaverse, describing the digital world as its "third address" (following two physical offices in Abu Dhabi and Dubai). The virtual headquarters is a multistorey building, each floor serving a different function (including a virtual conference space and meeting rooms). Visitors to the virtual HQ take a ticket on arrival, which prompts a government employee to join them in the metaverse. But what can visitors do at the virtual HQ? According to the Ministry, visitors can sign legally binding documents in the metaverse, eliminating the need to travel to one of the Ministry's physical locations.

This could also be an application for any corporate headquarters or event.

Attention to security remains a high priority for practitioners.[4]

We will have metaverse worlds indistinguishable from reality by 2030, and these realities will make the metaverse almost indistinguishable from the 'real' world.

The metaverse is no longer just a fantasy from science fiction novels. In recent years, it has become an increasingly popular topic of discussion and application in the real world. Many experts, Mark Zuckerberg aside, believe it will revolutionise how we interact, learn and engage with 'real' and digital content.

While the metaverse technically already exists in various forms, it is still in its infancy.

Once we move on from immersive games, we discover that several organisations are already 'in the metaverse'.

Existing examples like JP Morgan,[5] Volvo[6] and MasterCard[7] are there or thereabouts.

Here is a cure for managing the loss of banks in the high street: 'Banking in Metaverse – Launch Your Own Virtual Bank in the Metaverse' as seen on YouTube.

High-end brands such as Tommy Hilfiger, Gucci and Dolce & Gabbana have all invested millions of dollars into 'metaverse storefronts' and 'digital fashion'. More affordable brands such as Gap, Aeropostale and Forever 21 have created digital wardrobes for gaming platforms.

Decentralised metaverses utilise blockchain (see below) and decentralised storage to distribute as much of the digital environment as possible over many servers. This is when the metaverse movement intersects with the Web3 movement (see below). By decentralising the environment, no single party controls it, and users can own the data they generate.

These solutions will not only unlock massive new worlds of possibilities for businesses but could also lead to entirely new ways of interacting within digital spaces. These evolving technologies can be used to create immersive experiences or even entire virtual cities that allow users to work in an extensive environment that will fully engage stakeholders.

Because the metaverse is so immersive, it provides new and more compelling relationship-building capabilities. A metaverse creator EWG has some great demonstrations. Meta offers virtual workrooms ready for practitioners to create a board meeting.

New creative expression methods have emerged through 3D modelling programs like Blender and VR sculpting tools like Tilt Brush.

Overall, the metaverse transforms people's communication and interaction by providing new opportunities to explore digital space together. It has enabled us to experience new forms of communication that break down geographic boundaries while creating immersive communities that transcend physical limitations.

Traditional forms of communication, such as emails and phone calls, are becoming increasingly ineffective for businesses, but immersive forms of relationship building are becoming quite addictive (ask any teenager).

Companies need new ways to communicate with customers, partners and employees that are more efficient, engaging and relationship-building. In addition, they need the means to model new products, new social and economic environments, political change and international relations (virtual, real and combined).

This new form of communication could revolutionise PR. The metaverse is a space for PR people to work in now and to watch development for the future.

For most practitioners, the metaverse is not for now, but it is worth maintaining an interest in for tomorrow.

NOTES

1 Metaverse beyond the hype: Multidisciplinary perspectives on emerging challenges, opportunities, and agenda for research, practice and policy.
2 How do the news media, academia, and the public view the metaverse? Evidence from South Korea
    Science Direct
    https://www.sciencedirect.com/science/article/abs/pii/S00401625 23006650.
3 https://www.statista.com/outlook/amo/metaverse/metaverse-live-entertainment/united-kingdom.
4 Pooyandeh, M., Han, K.-J. and Sohn, I. (2022) 'Cybersecurity in the AI-based Metaverse: A survey', *Applied Sciences*, 12(24), p. 12993. doi: 10.3390/app122412993.
5 https://www.cxotoday.com/blockchain/jp-morgan-bets-on-metaverse-paving-way-for-virtual-banking/.
6 https://unity.com/case-study/volvo.
7 https://www.mastercard.com/news/perspectives/2022/building-the-metaverse/.

CHAPTER 13

APIs

A Completely New Medium

Tʜᴇʀᴇ ɪs ᴀ ᴄᴏᴍᴍᴜɴɪᴄᴀᴛɪᴏɴ medium that most PR practitioners simply don't know about.

It is a well-established technology. Most organisations use it, most media use it, many competitors are out there using it and it affects many important websites, if not the majority.

It is an Application Programming Interface (API)

How can the PR industry tap into this vast medium? How can practitioners harness this massively important technology?

It has two aspects: making outbound easy to collect and making information on the internet easy to acquire in real time.

This medium, hidden in plain sight, is a set of rules defining how two software programs can communicate online. It allows different applications to talk to each other and share data.

A web application is a software application hosted on a web server and delivered to users through a web browser. Web applications are typically used for tasks such as browsing the web, checking email, shopping online and managing finances.

Organisations use APIs and web applications in a variety of ways. For example, an organisation might use an API to integrate its customer relationship management (CRM) system with its e-commerce platform. This would allow the organisation to track customer orders and interactions across both systems. Or, an organisation might use a web application to

DOI: 10.1201/9781003507901-13

provide employees access to company resources, such as employee directories, HR information and training materials.

APIs and web applications can benefit organisations, including PR teams. Here are some specific examples of how PR teams can use APIs and web applications:

APIs are a crucial part of developing websites and establishing an online presence, and they can be an excellent resource for PR (Public Relations) practitioners for several reasons:

Enhanced User Experience: APIs allow websites to integrate with various external services, such as Anthropic's Claude, a potent and effective AI solution. Then, there are social media platforms, payment gateways and content delivery networks. This integration can enhance the user experience, making the website more engaging and dynamic.

Data Access: APIs provide access to data and functionality that can be valuable for PR practitioners. They can access real-time data from social media platforms, news sources or analytics tools, helping them stay informed about trends, mentionsand news related to their brand or industry.

Content Syndication: PR practitioners can syndicate content to various platforms using APIs. For example, they can automate the sharing of press releases, blog posts or news articles to multiple social media channels or news aggregators.

Analytics and Insights: APIs can retrieve analytics and performance data from websites and online platforms. This data is essential for PR practitioners to measure the impact of their campaigns, track engagement and make data-driven decisions.

Automation: APIs enable automation of various tasks. PR practitioners can use APIs to automate email marketing campaigns, social media posting and other repetitive tasks, saving time and ensuring consistency.

Custom Reporting: With APIs, PR practitioners can create custom reports and dashboards that consolidate data from various sources. This allows them to tailor their reporting to specific client or stakeholder needs.

Real-time Communication: APIs facilitate real-time communication with audiences. PR practitioners can use chatbots and messaging

APIs to engage with customers or journalists, providing immediate responses to inquiries or comments.

Content Distribution: APIs can be used to distribute content to media outlets and news aggregators, streamlining the process of getting news and press releases in front of journalists and the public.

Competitive Analysis: By accessing APIs from competitors' websites and social media accounts, PR practitioners can gain insights into their strategies, allowing for better positioning and response.

Innovation: PR practitioners can leverage APIs to stay at the forefront of technology trends. They can explore emerging platforms and technologies to find new ways to engage with audiences and tell their brand's story.

APIs play a crucial role in modern web development and online presence, offering PR practitioners valuable tools to enhance their strategies, stream-line processes, and stay informed about developments in their industry. Using APIs effectively can help PR professionals be more agile and responsive in today's fast-paced digital landscape.

APIs are becoming a significant development in communication, and applications are growing fast. Not the least is using APIs to act as a resource for AI engines. They are a readymade resource to provide instant transfer of information.

Here are some specific examples of how organisations use APIs and web applications:

- 'Clipping'/monitoring agencies use APIs to receive the latest published content made available by news outlets.

- Banks use APIs to allow customers to check their balances, transfer money and pay bills online.

- Retailers use APIs to allow customers to track their orders, make returns and redeem rewards.

- Travel companies use APIs to allow customers to book flights, hotels and rental cars.

- Logistics companies use APIs to track shipments and manage inventory.

- Media companies use APIs to allow users to stream videos and music.

Brewery and pub chain BrewDog implemented an API to improve customer engagement. They created a mobile app that allows customers to find the nearest BrewDog bar, order drinks and receive special offers. The API integrates with their point-of-sale system and loyalty programme, providing a seamless experience for customers and valuable data for the company.

The fintech company Wise developed APIs to enable businesses to make international payments easily and at a lower cost. Middle-sized companies in the UK have integrated Wise's API into their financial systems, allowing them to send and receive money internationally with transparency and competitive exchange rates.

Trainline, the online ticketing platform, offers APIs that middle-sized travel companies in the UK can use to provide train booking services on their own websites and apps. This API integration helps these companies expand their offerings and reach a wider audience.

Food delivery service Deliveroo provides APIs to restaurants and middle-sized food businesses in the UK. These APIs allow businesses to easily manage their menu listings, receive and process orders and track deliveries through the Deliveroo platform.

These are just a few examples, and as these technologies become even more common, we can expect to see even more innovative and creative ways to use them.

So, why should a PR department not make press material, social media contributions, briefing documents and much more available using APIs?

But where might you find an API?

Well, The API for X (Twitter) (https://developer.twitter.com/en/docs/twitter-api),

Facebook (https://developers.facebook.com/products/),

Public Sector content (https://www.api.gov.uk/#uk-public-sector-apis),

National Health Service (https://developer.api.nhs.uk/nhs-api),

Football (https://www.sportmonks.com/football-api/),

Google (https://console.cloud.google.com/apis/library) or any of their other millions of APIs Then they can be added to the client content and make it up-to-date (by the minute) and irresistible.

There is more. Google provides an API conversation bot program the client can use to have AI conversations with customers (https://developers.google.com/apis-explorer). It is one of a considerable number of Google applications for practitioners to use.

This is a massive resource and is not an unusual facility. There are many vendors offering APIs similar to the Google list, and some of them are open-source (and thus free).

To provide an API resource for stakeholders, they can be made available to the general public or a selected audience.

Take, for example, the BBC. It offers a host of APIs for you to remix/mashup. The list of available services are at: (https://www.bbc.co.uk/developer/technology/apis.html). The Radio Programmes Schedule (BBC website) offers links you can add to your company website, blog or other online presence about programmes played on the BBC.

Examples include music linking to artists, and Wildlife Finder which publishes live information. Radio 1 has developed a plan to make all resources available in a variety of formats, depending on the nature of the resource: XML, Atom, RSS 2, JSON, YAML, RDF, iCal, are all useful to enrich web presence and can make them attractive because the content is live and up to date.

An API resource can be available to the general public or a selected audience. This can be achieved using various methods, such as:

- Public API: This is an API available to anyone who wants to use it. Developers often use public APIs to create applications that interact with the data or services provided by the API.

- Private API: This API is only available to a select group of users. Businesses often use private APIs to access their data or services to their partners or employees.

- Partner API: This API is available to a select group of partners. Businesses often use partner APIs to provide their partners access to their data or services to help them build applications or services that integrate with the business's products or services.

- Internal API: This API is only available to the internal users of an organisation. Businesses often use internal APIs to provide access to their data or services to their employees to help them build applications or services that support the business's operations.

The method used to make an API resource available will depend on the specific needs of the organisation or business providing the API. For example, a business that wants to make its data available to the general public might use a public API. In contrast, a business that wants to provide access to its data to its partners might use a partner API.

Here are some of the factors to consider when choosing a method for making an API resource available:

- The need to be seen as a transparent organisation, which is important when considering ethics (see below)

- The intended audience: Who do you want to be able to use the API?

- The security requirements: How secure does the API need to be?

- The cost: How much will it cost to make the API available?

- The ease of use: How easy will it be for users to use the API?

- The scalability: How scalable is the API?

Considering these factors, you can choose the best method for making an API resource available to your target audience.

The PR practitioner will want to access APIs from partners and third parties for various applications.

Some practitioners are great at doing this stuff but most are not but can use online tools that do most of the heavy lifting.

There are services that can help find and integrate APIs into a website:

1. API Marketplaces Services like RapidAPI, AWS Marketplace and APIs.guru maintain a library of APIs that can be searched through. They provide documentation and SDKs to integrate different APIs easily.

2. API Tools Services like Postman, Swagger and Apigee provide tools to search APIs, view docs, generate client code and quickly integrate APIs. Some also have monitoring and analytics features.

3. API Frameworks Frameworks like Apigee and MuleSoft provide an abstraction layer to easily call different APIs from client code without worrying about the underlying implementation.

4. API Wrappers Some services will wrap or proxy an API to simplify integration or overcome issues like CORS. They are useful when you want to integrate an API that doesn't have proper browser support.

5. Integration Platforms as a Service (iPaaS) Platforms like Boomi, Zapier and IFTTT help connect web services and APIs through a visual interface without writing code. They are useful for quick no code integrations.

6. Developer Communities Websites like GitHub, Stack Overflow and ProgrammableWeb can be great resources to find API recommendations from developers and see sample code for integration.

The choice depends on the use case, complexity of integration, need for monitoring/analytics and level of customisation needed. Both self-service marketplaces and managed API platforms can make API integration straightforward.

CHAPTER 14

Computer Games

Video Games Are a Popular Form of Entertainment
The UK video game market was worth £7.16 billion in 2021. Its user base is huge. The UK is a leading gaming hub in Europe, with a thriving video game industry. The popularity of video games has soared, with the number of gamers expected to reach 57.56 million by 2027, up from 51.21 million in 2023. Even before the global pandemic, gaming was already a mainstream pastime, and its popularity exploded in 2020. Currently, approximately 56% of the UK population engages in gaming across various devices, a significant increase from 39% in 2019. Yes, computer games are a big medium for PR people. Through these games, there are many ways practitioners can influence stakeholders.

This is a medium that the Public Relations (PR) sector must recognise. Computer games are a medium for the practitioner.

With technological advancements, computer games have evolved exponentially, becoming more immersive, interactive and engaging. Computer games are fun. In 2022, the number of video gamers worldwide stood at 3.03 billion.[1] As an industry, it is huge, can support a lot of development and is changing fast. Computer games are becoming a cross-over technology with virtual and meta reality.

Computer game PR communication is one of those areas that offers new jobs in the PR sector.

In-game communication content is a form of content that places messages, products or services within the virtual world of a video game. This type of content is similar to messaging in films and television, where the content exists within the universe of the characters. In-game advertising is

DOI: 10.1201/9781003507901-14

already becoming increasingly popular as a way to reach a large and engaged audience of gamers.

There are several advantages to in-game communication. First, it can be very effective in reaching a target audience. Gamers are typically highly engaged with the games they play, and they are more likely to pay attention to messaging that are placed within the game. Second, in-game content can be very creative and immersive. Practitioners can use the virtual world of the game to create unique and memorable experiences for gamers. Third, in-game content can be very effective in measuring results. Practitioners can track how many people see their messages and how many people click on them.

Despite its advantages, in-game messaging is not without its challenges. First, it can be difficult to create which is both effective and non-intrusive. PR people need to be careful not to disrupt the gameplay or make players feel like they are being bombarded with messaging. Second, in-game placement can be expensive. Advertisers need to pay a premium to place messaging in popular games. Third, in-game messages can be difficult to measure. It can be difficult to track how effective content is influencing gamers' purchasing decisions.

Video games are a diverse medium with a wide range of features. Some of the most common features include:

- Graphics: Video games can feature a variety of graphics, from simple 2D graphics to complex 3D graphics. The quality of the graphics can have a significant impact on the player's experience.

- Sound: Video games can feature a variety of sound effects and music. The sound can create an immersive experience and can also be used to convey information to the player.

- Gameplay: The gameplay is the core of a video game. It is the way that the player interacts with the game world. The gameplay can be simple or complex, and it can be based on various mechanics.

- Story: Many video games feature a story. The story can be told through cutscenes, dialogue or environmental storytelling. The story can help give the game a sense of purpose and motivate the player.

- Characters: Video games often feature characters that the player can interact with. The player can control the characters or they can be non-playable characters (NPCs). The characters can help bring the game world to life and provide the player with challenges and rewards.

- Challenge: Video games often present the player with challenges. These challenges can be physical, mental or emotional. The challenges can help keep the player engaged and provide a sense of accomplishment when they are overcome.

- Reward: Video games often reward the player for completing challenges. These rewards can be in the form of new items, abilities or knowledge. The rewards can motivate the player to continue playing and provide a sense of satisfaction when earned.

- Socialisation: Many video games allow players to socialise with each other. This can be done through online multiplayer games or social features like chat and forums. Socialisation helps players to connect and provides a sense of community. This is a useful tool for relationship creation and management.

These are just some of the most common features of video games. The specific features of a video game will vary depending on the genre and the developer.

Video games can serve a variety of functions. Video games are a form of entertainment that can provide hours of enjoyment. Depending on the game, they can be relaxing, challenging or exciting.

They can also be used to teach various subjects, such as history, science and math and the benefits of the client offering. They can also be used to teach problem-solving skills and critical thinking skills and are a way to socialise with friends and family. They can also be a way to meet new people from all over the world. Video games can be a way to destress and relax. They can provide a distraction from everyday problems and help relieve tension.

Computer games can help to develop problem-solving skills. Players often have to solve puzzles or overcome challenges to progress through the game. This can help improve players' critical thinking skills and ability to think creatively and can be a way to express creativity.

Players can often customise their characters and the world around them. They can also create their own levels or 'mods'.

It is a stretch, but some video games can be a way to exercise physically. For example, many fitness games require players to move their bodies.

Simulation and gaming have emerged as promising tools in crisis management, providing dynamic environments for education and research.

Users can get a lot of benefits from gaming. All video games have the potential to provide some form of entertainment, education or social interaction.

Games can be used for different purposes, showing how PR people can adapt this media to interact with users.

So now we have to move from games and benefits to how PR can use this medium.

Computer games often have the means to contact players embedded in the game itself. This can be done through a variety of methods, such as:

- In-game chat: This is the most common way to communicate with other players in a game. Players can type messages to each other in real time, which can be a great way to coordinate strategies or just chat about the game.

- Text chat: This is a less common way to communicate with other players, but it can be useful for games that do not have in-game chat. Players can type messages to each other through a separate chat client, such as Discord or TeamSpeak.

- Voice chat: This is a more immersive way to communicate with other players but can also be more disruptive. Players can speak to each other in real time through a microphone, which can be useful for games that require teamwork.

- Social media: Many games have a social media presence, such as a X (Twitter) account or a Discord server (https://discord.com/servers). This can be a great way to communicate with players outside the game and be used to promote the game to new players.

- Email: Some games allow players to email each other directly. This can be a useful way to communicate with offline players simultaneously.

Using APIs is another way to communicate with players in a game. APIs are rules that allow two pieces of software to communicate. There are many APIs available for games, and they can be used to do things like:

- Automatically add content from websites and other online properties (even other games)

- Send push notifications to players
- Collect data about player behaviour
- Integrate with social media platforms
- Create custom game features

APIs can be a powerful way to communicate with players in a game. However, it is essential to use them carefully and ethically. For example, getting players' consent before collecting data about them is important.

APIs play a crucial role in video game development, enabling developers to access and integrate various data, rules, specifications and settings. These APIs facilitate communication between different applications, operating systems and libraries, allowing for seamless embedding and sharing of gaming content.

The diverse functionalities of APIs cater to a wide range of game development needs. Some APIs are specifically designed for graphics and sound management, while others address artificial intelligence requirements. This versatility highlights the profound impact of APIs on the gaming landscape.

APIs empower game developers to create immersive and engaging gaming experiences, catering to the diverse preferences of gamers worldwide.

Many educational video games are available, such as 'Minecraft Education Edition', which can teach students about various subjects, such as history, science and mathematics. There is a growing range of educational games.

Video games like 'Fortnite' and 'Animal Crossing' are popular for socialising with friends and family and client organisations. These games allow players to interact with each other in real time, either through voice chat or text chat.

It is important to note that the effects of video games on individuals can vary depending on various factors, such as the player's age, the type of game and the amount of time spent playing. However, video games can be a positive force in people's lives. They can provide entertainment, education and social interaction and help improve problem-solving skills, creativity and physical fitness.

Through Augmented Reality (AR), gamers can experience a virtual world superimposed on the real world.

However, before immersing ourselves in computer games, it is essential to understand what they are and their genres.

Computer games are a form of art that involves design, coding and storytelling to create a virtual world for players to explore. Computer games are interactive and rely on the player's direct or indirect participation. Computer games can range from solo-play games to massively multiplayer online games (MMOs).

There are several genres of computer games, each with its unique characteristics and gameplay.

The most popular activities can offer the communicator a basis for creating their games, sponsorship and offering new characters. Other game elements are similar to fast-paced gameplay, which challenges reflexes and problem-solving skills and typically involves combat, often focusing on melee combat rather than guns. Adventure games usually focus on interactive storytelling, with the player exploring an open-world environment and solving puzzles. Sports games often simulate real-life sports, with players competing against each other or the game AI. Racing games that involve vehicles, bikes or boats can also be the basis for PR games communication.

Computer games in 2023 took on a new role by becoming a spatial computer that allows users to be present and socially connected while seamlessly fusing digital material with the real environment.

The Apple Vision Pro[2] is a gaming headset that presents a fully three-dimensional user interface controlled by the most natural and intuitive inputs – a user's eyes, hands and voice – and creates an infinite canvas for programmes that expand beyond the limitations of a traditional computer games display. Vision Pro allows consumers to engage with digital information in a way that makes it feel like it is physically present in their location, thanks to the VisionOS operating system offering what Apple calls a spatial operating system. The key element of the VisionOS launch was that it did not mention computer games. It was positioned in the metaverse and not in the computer gaming genre.

In 2023, it was positioned for broader audiences, including the business community.

In the meantime it is worth looking at some interesting applications.

- Lloyds Banking Group: Lloyds Banking Group has used computer games to train its employees. The game 'The Virtual Bank' allows employees to learn about the bank's products and services in a safe and interactive environment.

- Shell: Shell has used computer games to raise awareness about climate change. The game 'Climate Challenge' allows players to learn about the causes and effects of climate change and what they can do to help.

- The National Health Service (NHS): The NHS has used computer games to help patients manage their health. The game 'My Diabetes Coach' allows patients with diabetes to learn how to manage their condition.

- The British Army: The British Army has used computer games to train its soldiers. The game 'Operation Flashpoint' allows soldiers to learn about combat tactics and weapons in a safe and realistic environment.

These are just a few examples of how British companies use computer games for communication. As technology continues to evolve, we can expect to see even more innovative and creative ways to use games to communicate with others.

In addition to these companies, many independent game developers in the UK are creating games that have a social or educational purpose. The use of computer games for communication is still in its early stages, but it has the potential to be a powerful tool for educating, training and engaging people. As technology develops, we can expect to see even more innovative and creative ways to use games to communicate with others.

There is a considerable corpus of research into the nature and effectiveness of computer games.[3]

Computer games are often associated with entertainment, but they also have some surprising applications in business. Games can be a valuable tool for companies looking to gain a competitive edge, from improving employee performance to increasing customer engagement.

Another way in which computer games can be used in business is in PR, marketing and advertising.

Deloitte created a virtual reality game that helps new hires learn about their organisational structure, work culture and existing projects. Companies like Coca-Cola and Burger King have created games as a marketing strategy. These games are designed to engage customers in fun and interactivity while promoting their products and services. For example, Coca-Cola created a game called 'Happiness Quest', where players had to guide a character around different scenarios, collecting red discs representing happiness. Once enough discs are collected, a coupon for a free Coke is released. This game was highly successful in customer engagement and helped enhance the company's image as a fun and innovative brand.

Some games allow up-to-the-minute and real data from external sources (using APIs).

Integrating real-time data (see below) into computer games means game developers can access the most up-to-date information in real time. For example, if a game is based on current news, events or sports results, this information can be easily accessed through API integration. Such integrations enable practitioners to keep their games up to date with minimal effort – something that would otherwise be incredibly time-consuming if done manually.

Computer games can also be used in HR to help increase employee engagement and productivity. An example of a platform that leverages gamification to improve performance management is BetterWorks, where employees can set goals, track progress and receive rewards for achieving milestones.

Some practitioners may want to create their own games for specific purposes. School and university classes are a great way to access and provide immersive content.

Games can also be used for data analysis and visualisation. Several examples of companies have taken data analysis a step further by creating games that allow users to interact with data in a fun and engaging way. For instance, IBM Watson Analytics, a cognitive data analysis software, has an interesting feature called 'Explore'. The feature allows users to explore their data through (often AI generated) exploration games. These games take players on a journey through their data, and as they progress, they receive new insights and visualisations that help them to make better decisions based on their data.

Companies like Coca-Cola, Deloitte, Betterworks and IBM Watson have successfully leveraged the power of gaming technology in their business applications. Modelling issues and crisis management are further applications available for PR planning.

We expect to see more companies embrace the concept of gamification in their operations. Agencies and organisations will be using universities to help develop games for these interesting applications.

To learn how to build computer games is difficult and will take an account executive a full weekend using a Google search for 'open source computer games software for beginners'. The beginner should play with free, open-source software to find their way around the nature of computer games and computer game development and then apply it internally first.

Game development takes time, so it's important to be organised and have a plan. Here are the steps for developing a computer game:

> Conceptualise the game and start brainstorming ideas for your target audience/s, what type of game it will be, what features it will have, etc. You can also use existing concepts as inspiration or create something entirely new. This is a mature form of infotainment, so a wide range of software is available to help design and develop specific and bespoke games.[4]

Design the Game – once you know what your game should look like, you can begin designing it. This involves creating character designs, levels, rules, mechanics, etc., all the while keeping in mind your target audience and overall goal for the game. You don't need fancy software; pen and paper work just fine!

Next comes programming your game using a language such as C++ or Java. This step requires knowledge of coding principles to create logic that allows your game to function properly. It can be daunting, but with enough practice, anyone can learn how to code their games – but it takes work!

Before releasing the finished product into the wild (or even during development), testing the game for bugs and glitches that could hamper player experiences later on is important. Testing involves playing the game multiple times with different scenarios to find any issues that may arise during gameplay.

The idea is that using game development software is only for gamers to think again. It is a great way to describe products, ideas and environments. Quite often, there is a need to search and integrate external data, which can act as a news vendor or update client information.

Integrating artificial intelligence (AI) techniques and technologies into video games has gained significant traction recently. AI in gaming is beginning to revolutionise the player experience by enhancing the realism, immersion and dynamic nature of gameplay.

One of the key advantages of AI in gaming is the ability to create more intelligent and responsive computer-controlled opponents. Instead of using prescribed behaviours, AI-powered opponents can adapt and make decisions based on the player's actions, creating a more challenging and engaging gameplay experience. These opponents can analyse the player's strategies, learn from their mistakes and adjust their behaviour accordingly, making each encounter feel unique and tailored to the player's skills.

AI in gaming communication and business modelling can also be used to create more realistic and lifelike worlds. AI-controlled NPCs can exhibit complex and believable behaviours, such as interacting with the environment, reacting to stimuli (often using APIs) and simulating human-like social interactions. This adds depth and improves the overall immersion for users.

Furthermore, AI can be used to enhance game design and development processes. With AI systems capable of generating content, such as levels, characters and narratives, game developers can streamline their workflow and create more varied and dynamic gameplay experiences. AI can also be used for playtesting, allowing developers to identify flaws, balance gameplay and optimise the player experience.

The ongoing advancements in AI, particularly in areas like machine learning and neural networks, provide new opportunities for innovative game design and AI companions. With breakthroughs like reinforcement learning, AI can become more adaptive and self-improving, enabling game characters to learn and evolve.

The hype around AI in gaming is justified by its potential to transform the gaming industry and provide users with more immersive and personalised experiences. As AI technology continues to evolve, we can expect even more exciting advancements in integrating AI in video games, pushing the boundaries of what's possible in terms of gameplay, storytelling and player engagement.

NOTES

1 Clement, J. (2023) *Global video game users 2027, Statista*. Available at: https://www.statista.com/statistics/748044/number-video-gamers-world/ (Accessed: 16 June 2023).
2 *Introducing apple vision pro: Apple's first Spatial Computer* (2023) *Apple Newsroom (United Kingdom)*. Available at: https://www.apple.com/uk/newsroom/2023/06/introducing-apple-vision-pro/ (Accessed: 16 June 2023).
3 Pötzsch, H., Hansen, T.H. and Hammar, E.L. (2023) 'Digital Games as media for teaching and learning: A template for critical evaluation', *Simulation & Gaming*, p. 104687812311662. doi:10.1177/10468781231166213.
4 *10 best video game design & development software 2023* (2023) *Software Testing Help*. Available at: https://www.softwaretestinghelp.com/best-game-development-software (Accessed: 22 June 2023).

CHAPTER 15

Find and Analyse Coverage

W E HAVE BEEN THROUGH so many media changes in less than two centuries. Mass communications with radio and TV, the advent of computer discs, data assembly and then the internet all had big effects. The internet, websites, Usenet and social media are now common and largely used by the whole population. Mobile phones and the many media they support are in every pocket or handbag.

All these media are driven by and collect data.

The vast amount of data accumulated so far is like the grains of sand on the biggest beach in the world and encompasses nearly all the information and knowledge known to mankind.

Practitioners may want to keep current on a particular subject. There are, of course, news scraping search engines like Google and Bing, but they have had to develop fast and be more sophisticated to compete with You.com and others driven by artificial intelligence search engines. As this book is being written, more such facilities are coming online. OpenAI began to offer custom versions of its services that allowed people to create their own tools and not more so than a few are monitoring online presence. The AI Actions by Zapier offers a wide range of opportunities.

A simple trick is available to find out which technologies are available. Find open-source (see: https://opensource.com/) and free services and explore what they do. This reveals what is here and what kinds of things they do[1] and will point to the more advanced and maybe costly alternatives.

 DOI: 10.1201/9781003507901-15

There is a lot of software to help, which includes text analysis, text mining and text analytics. They have become essential to PR account handlers as they deal with large amounts of data daily. Text analysis tools help analyse unstructured data[2] such as news articles, social media posts, customer feedback and more to identify patterns, sentiments and themes.

There are different types of software available.

Much of it is proprietary and can cost a lot of money; some offer free versions, yet others are open source.

Open-source software is a computer software in which the source code is released under an open-source licence, allowing anyone to use, modify and share the software. It can be used for various applications such as web development, programming language creation and content analysis.

However, with so many free software tools available, it can be difficult to know where to begin. Some suggestions are here, but there are others available.

Such capabilities are well within the competence of the PR practitioner to use.

With the help of these tools, PR account handlers can analyse unstructured data to gain new insights into their work and improve their impact.

By using such facilities, the practitioner enters the realm of Deep Learning.

The PR industry is well aware of the web scraping (search engine) tools used by the 'press cuttings' services. They monitor press media sites, social media and broadcast content mostly using API's.

They then offer 'magic' by analysing content for tone of content and more. This is not hard. The AI software is available to all practitioners, and the capabilities are very extensive.

In this book, there is a revelation. Are practitioners locked into some of the deeply disguised media such as computer games APIs, VR and AR, among others? Here, they are revealed.

Some, but by no means all, practitioners will want to delve into the underlying code behind many services. With code generation and debugging to its generative AI offering called Bard, Google now provides developers with a comprehensive programming and software development toolkit. Helping them create functions for Sheets (Google's spreadsheet service and part of its Doc service) and writing snippets in over 20 computer programming languages, including C++, Go Java, JavaScript, Python or TypeScript, enables users to accelerate their workflow while learning new capabilities. Analysts agree that these features will likely help further adoption of low-code platforms such as Microsoft's GitHub, Copilot and Amazon CodeWhisperer by letting coders explain what they wrote via an external platform – resulting in improved understanding across teams. Even computer coding is being automated by AI!

Bear in mind that practitioners need to be aware of the UK General Data Protection Regulation (see below) 2018.[3]

Some examples of tools that will offer insights to the practitioner follow.

GATE (General Architecture for Text Engineering) is a powerful graphical tool for building text processing pipelines. GATE can help analyse text for information extraction, sentiment analysis, machine translation and more. GATE offers support for many languages and platforms, making it a versatile tool for PR account handlers.

Orange is an open-source data visualisation and analysis tool that can also be used for text analysis. Orange offers a user-friendly interface that includes a range of visualisations and statistical analysis methods. Using Orange, PR account handlers can analyse text while also visualising the results in a clear and intuitive way.

RapidMiner: RapidMiner is an analytics platform that offers a range of data mining and machine learning tools. RapidMiner offers a text mining extension that allows PR account handlers to analyse unstructured data through methods such as topic modelling, sentiment analysis and more. RapidMiner is built on an open-source architecture, making it highly flexible and customisable.

WordStat: WordStat is a text analysis software tool specialising in content analysis, text analytics and text mining. WordStat features an intuitive interface and offers support for a range of languages. PR account handlers can use WordStat to analyse text for sentiment analysis, qualitative text analysis and more.

LingPipe: LingPipe is a natural language processing tool (NLP) focussed on text mining and analysis. LingPipe supports various languages and can be used for sentiment analysis, information extraction and more. LingPipe offers a Java API and a command-line interface, making it highly flexible for different analysis tasks.

OpenText Analytics: OpenText Analytics is a suite of software tools designed for text analytics and text mining. The suite includes modules for sentiment analysis, information extraction, automated categorisation and more. The suite is highly customisable and can be used on structured and unstructured data. It also offers support for a range of languages.

RavenPack: RavenPack is a professional-grade text analytics platform designed to help businesses make better decisions. The platform can be used for sentiment analysis, keyword extraction, social media monitoring and more. It supports multiple languages and includes advanced features like real-time streaming data processing and sophisticated visualisations. It also integrates with other business intelligence solutions.

IBM Watson: IBM Watson is an AI-powered platform that can help organisations analyse and interpret large datasets. It includes modules for text analytics and natural language processing, allowing users to quickly uncover insights from their data. Watson's features include the ability to recognise entities, concepts and sentiment in unstructured texts and machine learning capabilities for predictive analytics. It also includes advanced visualisation tools to help users explore data and gain insights more quickly.

Microsoft Azure: Microsoft Azure is a cloud computing service that provides analytics, database, storage and other services to customers. It offers a range of machine learning features, including automated prediction models and real-time analytics. Azure also provides tools for data scientists, including HDInsight and Data Science Virtual Machines, which allow customers to quickly set up and manage machine learning services in the cloud.

Amazon Web Services: Amazon Web Services (AWS) is a cloud computing platform that provides businesses a wide range of services, from storage to artificial intelligence capabilities.

The following was created by the Microsoft AI engine https://copilot. microsoft.com/👍

THE GENERAL DATA PROTECTION REGULATION (GDPR)

The General Data Protection Regulation (GDPR), which is implemented in the UK through the **Data Protection Act 2018**, holds significant importance for **Public Relations (PR) practitioners**. We need to be aware of the following:

1. **Legal compliance**:
   - The GDPR mandates strict rules for handling personal data. PR professionals must ensure that their practices align with these regulations.
   - By adhering to the GDPR, PR practitioners demonstrate legal compliance and protect both their clients and their own organisations from potential penalties.

2. **Transparency and accountability**:
   - The GDPR emphasises transparency in data processing. PR practitioners should be transparent about how they collect, use and share personal information.
   - Being accountable means maintaining clear records of data processing activities and ensuring that individuals' rights are respected.

3. **Data protection principles**:
   - PR professionals must follow the data protection principles outlined in the GDPR:
     - **Fair and lawful use**: Personal data should be used fairly, lawfully and transparently.
     - **Purpose limitation**: Data should be used only for specified, explicit purposes.
     - **Data minimization**: Use only relevant and necessary data.
     - **Accuracy and updates**: Keep data accurate and up-to-date.
     - **Storage limitation**: Retain data only as long as necessary.
     - **Security measures**: Ensure appropriate security to prevent unauthorised access or loss.

4. **Sensitive information**:
   - The GDPR provides stronger protection for sensitive data, including details related to:

- Race

- Ethnic background

- Political opinions

- Religious beliefs

- Trade union membership

- Genetics

- Biometrics (used for identification)

- Health

- Sex life or orientation

5. **Rights of individuals**:

- PR practitioners must respect individuals' rights under the GDPR:

  - **Access**: Individuals can request information about their data.

  - **Correction**: Incorrect data must be updated.

  - **Erasure**: Individuals can request data deletion.

  - **Restriction**: Individuals can limit data processing.

  - **Portability**: Data can be transferred to other services.

  - **Objection**: Individuals can object to certain data processing.

NOTES

1 Imanuel (2022) *Top 26 free software for text analysis, text mining, text analytics in 2022 reviews, features, pricing, comparison, PAT RESEARCH: B2B Reviews, Buying Guides & Best Practices*. Available at: https://www. predictiveanalyticstoday.com/top-free-software-for-text-analysis-text-mining-text-analytics/ (Accessed: 08 June 2023).

2 *Unstructured Data* (2023) *Wikipedia*. Available at: https://en.wikipedia.org/ wiki/Unstructured_data (Accessed: 08 June 2023).

3 *UK GDPR guidance and resources* (no date) *ICO*. Available at: https://ico.org. uk/for-organisations/uk-gdpr-guidance-and-resources/ (Accessed: 08 June 2023).

CHAPTER 16

Stakeholder Modelling

ONCE UPON A TIME, a century ago, communicators tried to identify stakeholders (also variously called publics and audiences – see below). Now, services such as Pulsar, Meltwater and Cision offer a range of capabilities that allow practitioners to identify and trace people, subject matter, timelines and much more. They also track trends and offer some form of prediction.

There are several benefits to using AI for stakeholder modelling. AI can help to identify stakeholders who may not be obvious at first glance. Computer intelligence can also help to collect and analyse data about stakeholders more quickly and efficiently than traditional methods. Additionally, using traditional methods, AI can generate insights about stakeholders that would be difficult or impossible to obtain otherwise.

However, some challenges are associated with using AI for stakeholder modelling. One challenge is that AI models can be biased, and it is important to consider the data used to train them carefully. Additionally, AI models can be complex and difficult to understand, making it difficult to interpret the results of these models. But with effort and application, it becomes pretty easy.

Microsoft and Google have very large models (such as ChatGPT and Bard), which is familiar to PR practitioners. Still, some other models will be based on data collected from one or more APIs ('Application Programming Interface'), corporate databases or other sources and will not be the same.

Companies like Tesco offer insights into how they manage huge amounts of data to identify activity in stores to help triangulate insights

DOI: 10.1201/9781003507901-16

for primary research, contact centre feedback and external data partners to view a connected customer journey and make improvements where possible. They provide examples such as ....

> Suppose you must be a front-runner. In that case, you have to have such a connected data ecosystem, enabling Advanced Analytics and Machine Learning to find opportunities to create a better customer experience ahead of our competitors by a few days or weeks.

The Tesco resource about their research is worth reading.[1]

The activities of stakeholders offer serious competitive opportunities, and these data can be used in a number of ways. Today, there is a lot of useful academic study in the area.[2]

Today, we can identify clusters (cluster modelling) of people interested in organisations or products and entities that operate together with the range and strength of their interests and the strength of relationships between them. Some of these capabilities use AI to help, and some are also open source.[3] One such is One AI. Google, too, has AI-supported natural language processing and analysis capability.

Cluster modelling software[4] is a powerful tool that helps analyse and categorise large datasets. The software works by taking data and identifying similarities between data points using algorithms.

Extracting clean data to provide a database to model such as Twitter relationships (subjects, people relationships, hashtags etc.[5]). The same approach is possible for Twitter, Facebook and other online interactions, where an API[6] is available to download data.

Cluster modelling has many applications. In its dynamic mode, it offers insights into the key stakeholders and their relationships, notably to the organisation. The capability identifies different stakeholders' opinions, products, culture and service impressions over time and, to a time-decaying extent, into the future. It predicts interested stakeholders, their relationships (clusters) and the topics of interest.

This knowledge can inform the development of products and services and has the prospect of automating other forms of research, market and competitor analysis and underlying business needs.

Stakeholder modelling using artificial intelligence identifies and analyses the stakeholders involved in a project or initiative. AI can collect and analyse stakeholder data, including their interests, goals and potential impact on the project. This information can then be used to develop

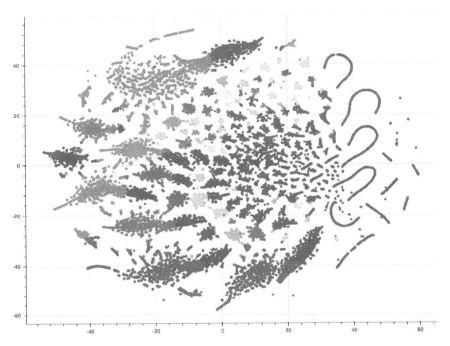

Bogdanowicz, A. and Guan, C. (no date) 'Dynamic topic modelling of Twitter data during the COVID-19 pandemic', *PLOS One*. Available at: https://journals. plos.org/plosone/article?id=10.1371%2Fjournal.pone.0268669 (Accessed: 16 June 2023).

strategies for engaging and managing stakeholders throughout the project lifecycle.

There are many benefits to using AI for stakeholder modelling. AI can help to identify stakeholders who may not be obvious at first glance, and it can also help to collect and analyse data about stakeholders more quickly and efficiently than traditional methods. Additionally, AI can generate insights about stakeholders that would be difficult or impossible to obtain otherwise.

The process is not too hard. There is a need to identify the API/s you need, for example, X (Twitter), LinkedIn, Facebook, Instagram, Google searches etc. and download the references you need. It is then possible to mine these data for relevant content (the client?). Then get the AI engine to collect data such as date/time attitude, and relationships between actors and with the organisation. This can then be displayed as a table or chats and run in time sequences to show changes in relationships over time (and can be displayed as an augmented reality or a dynamic cluster model display).

This then is how the PR person can watch the effects of clients, competitors or third-party activity on stakeholders.

Then there is the problem that many practitioners face: The unknown unknowns (*unk uks*). Who are the people who are not evident online, who do not use social media or eschew the client but not its competitors? The practitioner needs to know who these people are and how to build relationships with them. Such actors need to be considered before ignoring such people.

When I use the term stakeholder it means: organisations chosen stakeholders by their marketing strategies, recruiting and investment plans, but 'publics' arise on their own and choose the organisation for attention.[7] Also, clientele, audience, followers, congregation, community etc.

NOTES

1 Pereira, D. (2023) *Tesco Swot Analysis (2023), Business Model Analyst*. Available at: https://businessmodelanalyst.com/tesco-swot-analysis/ (Accessed: 16 June 2023).

2 Miller, G. J. (2022) 'Stakeholder roles in artificial intelligence projects', *Project Leadership and Society*, 3, p. 100068. doi: 10.1016/j.plas.2022.100068.

3 Open-source licenses, which are available in various forms, give users the freedom to use, distribute and modify the software. Anyone can use the software without any cost, and developers can adapt and modify the code, even extending and building on it through a community-driven approach. The open-source approach enables users to learn from, share, contribute and collaborate with others.

   The biggest advantage of open-source software is that it empowers individuals and organisations to work together and create solutions that nobody alone could create. The open-source software model encourages innovation, greater interoperability, faster development cycles and greater flexibility. The result is that code is created and shared freely by the community, and anyone can benefit from it.

4 https://github.com/DocNow/hydrator.

5 *Topic modeling of twitter followers* (2015) *Alexis Perrier – Data Science*. Available at: https://alexisperrier.com/nlp/2015/09/04/topic-modeling-of-twitter-followers (Accessed: 16 June 2023).

6 https://en.wikipedia.org/wiki/API.

7 Grunig, J. E., & Repper, F. C. (1992). Strategic management, publics, and issues. In J. E. Grunig (Ed.), Excellence in public relations and communication management (pp. 117–158). Lawrence Erlbaum Associates.

CHAPTER 17

Data Integration

IN THE REALM OF data management and analysis, the integration of various sources of information, such as databases and spreadsheets, using Artificial Intelligence (AI) has become a pivotal aspect of modern business operations.

This chapter will delve into the ways AI can be harnessed to amalgamate diverse datasets, with a focus on British applications that exemplify best-in-class practices.

The amalgamation of databases, spreadsheets and other sources of information has always been a fundamental challenge for businesses aiming to extract valuable insights from their data. In recent years, the integration of AI technologies has provided a powerful solution to this age-old problem. By automating data consolidation and analysis, AI streamlines decision-making processes, enhances productivity and fosters innovation.

AI plays a pivotal role in data integration by automating the process of harmonising diverse datasets. Through techniques such as Natural Language Processing (NLP), Machine Learning (ML), and Data Mining, AI can analyse data from various sources and transform it into a unified format.

AI-powered algorithms can identify inconsistencies, errors and duplications within databases and spreadsheets. For instance, British healthcare applications like "NHS Digital" employ AI to clean and standardise patient records, ensuring data accuracy for healthcare providers.

An example is in public records about people. Most people have a National Insurance number. It is used to make sure your National Insurance contributions and tax are recorded against your name only.

DOI: 10.1201/9781003507901-17

Your NHS number is unique to you. It helps healthcare staff and service providers identify you correctly and match your details to your health records. When you visit a hospital, you will get another hospital number. Dentists, opticians, pharmacists, paediatricians and other health service providers also hold your details on different systems, each with their own numbering system. How, then, does a front-line GP get to know all the details needed to diagnose a patient with watering eyes, a headache, decaying teeth and a baby on her lap? There are similar data jungles for almost all government departments.

The NHS is spending a fortune trying to bring all these data together. But it's more complex. How, for example, can patient confidentiality be maintained or how can one institution trust the validity of another's inputs and so the debates go on.

AI algorithms enable the seamless integration of data from different software platforms. British financial institutions like Barclays utilise AI-powered middleware to combine data from legacy systems with modern databases, enabling a holistic view of customer financial information.

NLP algorithms enable AI to understand the meaning and context of data. British media companies like the BBC leverage AI to analyse viewer interactions with content across various platforms, tailoring content recommendations and personalising user experiences.

AI can enhance datasets by adding contextual information. British e-commerce giants like ASOS use AI to enrich product listings with customer reviews and social media sentiment analysis, providing valuable insights into consumer preferences.

AI-driven predictive analytics, as seen in British energy companies like National Grid, can forecast trends by analysing data from multiple sources, optimising energy distribution and reducing costs.

Today, what was once only available to big organisations is available to much smaller institutions.

Data integration solutions can be extended to other departments in the organisation, enabling cross-functional collaboration to be easily achieved. In addition, data integration can help detect and prevent errors due to inconsistencies between different datasets. This means that businesses can rely on accurate information when making decisions.

A single access to information is an invaluable resource for businesses that want to improve their operations and gain a competitive advantage. By accessing accurate, up-to-date data, businesses can make informed decisions that drive positive outcomes. Furthermore, data integration also saves time and money, as it automates many manual processes and eliminates the need for multiple systems.

The problem is that organisational data is held all over the place. The lists and databases, spreadsheets and calendars are all data that can be valuable. Today we have a great asset to help explore all these data sources: artificial intelligence.

Data Integration also has relevance for public relations practitioners. With the right data integration platform, practitioners can quickly and easily tap into customer data from social media to identify key stakeholders interested in their products or services. This creates a great opportunity for practitioners to build relationships with these key stakeholders and create opportunities for collaboration. Furthermore, this data can be used to customise campaigns and messages specifically tailored towards the interests of each stakeholder/group, making it more likely to receive a positive response. Data integration can also help practitioners identify new relationship opportunities and trends they may have missed.

Using ChatGPT the author asked the AI to identify the presence of the name in a spreadsheet. The response was:

> To search for entries related to 'David' across all sheets, I'll go through each sheet in the Excel file, look for mentions of 'David', and compile a list of any findings, including the sheet name (which represents the month) and any relevant details. This process will provide a comprehensive overview of 'David's' involvement. Let's start this search.
>
> Entries related to 'David' were found in several sheets. Here's a summary of the findings, including the sheet name and details:
>
> - *May 2023*:
>   - On Trinity 2, 11.00 am, Morning Prayer service, David/ Margaret Philipps are mentioned under the column possibly related to attendance or roles, with xxxxxx also mentioned.
> - *MarApr 2023 (March/April 2023)*:
>   - In an 11.00 am service for Holy Communion, David/ Margaret Phillips are mentioned, with xxxxxxx/yyyyyyyy and zzzzzzzz also noted.

- *JanFeb 2023*:
  - *During an 11.00 am Morning Prayer service, David/ Margaret Phillips are mentioned, with xxxxxxxxx and aaaaaaa also listed.*

    These entries suggest that David (alongside Margaret Philipps/Phillips) is involved in various capacities across different months. The roles or specific activities are not entirely clear from the summary but likely relate to participation in services or responsibilities within those services.

It would have been easy to point ChatGPT to several spreadsheets, databases and APIs and to use more sophisticated capabilities. But it just takes a minute or two, and there are many other AI engines that can be used.

This is a powerful tool for public relations practitioners looking to increase their reach and generate valuable insights about their target stakeholders. By tapping into customer data, as well as leveraging social media channels, practitioners can gain really useful information.

Through data integration, public relations practitioners can go beyond identifying stakeholders and venture into understanding their relationships and interests. Leveraging data from LinkedIn, X, Facebook and most other social media, they can uncover connections between stakeholders, map out networks of influence and gain insights into these individuals' topics and industries of interest.

This intelligence is invaluable in creating highly targeted public relations strategies that resonate with stakeholders, thus fostering meaningful relationships based on shared interests and mutual benefit. By understanding and addressing the unique needs and concerns of each stakeholder, public relations practitioners can ensure their message hits the mark every time, thereby enhancing the effectiveness of their communication efforts.

This interrogation of information can also be used to populate outputs such as web pages or social media.

For the public relations practitioner, the advantage of having a single explorable and available source is great for identifying information needed. Much of these data can be fed directly into other databases, web pages, imagery and even videos for briefings, websites and social media publications.

CHAPTER 18

Networking and Computers make Friends

NETWORKING IS ONE OF the joys and pleasures of public relations. We do a lot of it. It is a powerful way of building relationships, identifying needs and interests and spotting social networks in a social environment. It is the most ancient form of communication and it is still relevant today.

Social networks are an essential part of life in the 21st century. They allow us to connect with friends, family, colleagues and even strangers from all over the world. Not all social networks are person-to-person; computer-aided social networks can be used for a variety of purposes.

Seeking out networks is now part of PR. Networks include people with similar interests (see the chapter about data integration), which can provide PR intelligence and identify key stakeholders and message frameworks. Of course, this has to be done with care. Interfering with the dynamic of a network will be a reputational disaster.

Staying connected using social networks makes it easy to stay in touch with stakeholders both near and far away.

The evolution of dynamic relationship building is getting powerful tools. The days of a 'little black book' of contacts is long gone.

Sharing data and updates about a client and even video chats are part of the current mix. This is co-existence with the virtual world(s). Zoom, Teams and Google Meet are commonly used, but now there are new options using gaming programmes and much more. Virtual and

DOI: 10.1201/9781003507901-18

augmented reality conferences are becoming great ways to interact (even the United Nations uses these technologies).

Social networks can be a great way to build professional relationships. You can connect with colleagues, potential employers and industry leaders. You can also use social networks to share your work and expertise and to learn about new opportunities.

These networks can be a great source of support and advice, including people who are experts or are going through similar experiences.

This form of communication is also a great way to learn new things. You can follow experts in your field, join groups that share your interests, attend virtual lectures and take online courses.

This is such a good way of having fun too. You can play games, watch videos and listen to music. You can also use social networks to meet new people and make friends.

Building social networks in the 21st century is essential for success both personally and professionally.

Social networking is changing.

Social networks have become more personalised and tailored to the interests and needs of each user. This is done using AI and Machine Learning (ML).

Social networks are becoming more immersive, allowing users to interact with each other more realistically. This is already done through VR and AR.

Social networks can become more decentralised, with users having more control over their data and privacy. This will be done using blockchain technology (see below).

We use networking to build relationships and create a strong personal brand for ourselves, our employers and the organisations we work with. It is also useful for staying ahead of trends in the industry and sourcing information about new products, services and solutions.

Of course, we have a lot of new social networking aids. WhatsApp, Zoom, Twitter, Instagram and hundreds of other social media platforms are recent forms of networking. They will evolve. Already it's possible to hold conversations with bots.[1] Amica is a humanoid robot developed by Engineered Arts.[2] It is the most advanced humanoid robot in the world, and it is still under development. However, it can potentially be a very capable companion in the future.

In health, there are a lot of uses for this kind of interface, and robot nurses and surgeons are close enough. As conference receptionists, they are potentially magical.

Within five years, Ameca is expected to be able to hold conversations, remember people and their interests and become a very companionable person at a reception. It will be able to do this by combining AI and ML. Ameca's AI will allow it to understand human language and respond in a natural way in any language or dialect. It will also be able to learn from its interactions with people to improve its conversation skills over time.

Wearable devices are becoming increasingly popular, and many of them now include facial recognition cameras. These cameras can be used for a variety of purposes, including:

- Security: Facial recognition can be used to unlock devices, grant access to buildings or even identify people in crowds.

- Payment: Facial recognition can be used to make payments without having to carry a physical wallet or credit card.

- Health: Facial recognition can be used to monitor health data, such as heart rate, sleep patterns and stress levels.

- Social: Facial recognition can be used to connect with friends and family or to share photos and videos.

Camera glasses are special glasses with a camera inside. They can help us recognise stakeholders, and whisper who you are meeting in your ear. Never forget the name of anyone ever again!

The range of tools available to enhance relationships and relationship management is extensive.

NOTES

1 https://en.wikipedia.org/wiki/Chatbot
2 https://www.engineeredarts.co.uk/robot/ameca/

CHAPTER 19

Brain to Computer

S O FAR WE HAVE written about PR communication that is firmly in the mid-20s. It's time for some fun.

Originally this chapter was to be at the end of the book because brain to computer communication seemed so far off. It's not!

Communication has changed a lot in the past, but even more exciting changes are coming. They are definitely in the realm of relations management and communication.

It is developing very fast now, but what about some groundbreaking stuff:

Brain-to-brain communication?

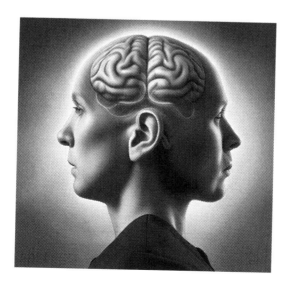

DOI: 10.1201/9781003507901-19

It is only for a few practitioners now. But it could become mainstream as we grasp the metaverse and other emerging technologies over the next five years or so.

Brain to Computer Communication (BCC) is a rapidly evolving field of research in neuroscience and computer science. It is opening up a new form of communication. It seeks to develop technologies that allow humans to interact directly with computers using their brains. BCC is based on the idea that neurons, or brain cells, can be used to send signals to a computer, allowing users to control the machine without any physical input. The technology also allows computers to interpret signals sent by the brain and provide feedback in real time.

This idea is no farther away from science fiction than one might imagine. We already have it. We have skin to computer. It's common—a tiny wearable computer worn as a watch on many wrists worldwide. They monitor pulse, ECG, blood pressure, the number of steps and even the user's location. These data are often shared with other computers and even others' watches. The location of friends can be displayed on another watch. Levels of anxiety and excitement, temperature and interest in information (including news) are also monitored.

All this is frequently transmitted in real time to other computers and computer networks. This is your information, but who owns the data once it has been moved to a third-party computer? Where are the ethics police?

So far, so good. But we know that computers communicate with each other. These processors may also be able to communicate with a second person thousands of miles away. If we take this idea further, how many people can be included in this data conversation?

The development of this technology has been built upon understanding how the human brain works and its ability to transmit electrical information through neuron pathways. Scientists measure these signals from outside the body using non-invasive imaging techniques such as electroencephalography (EEG), magnetoencephalography (MEG), functional magnetic resonance imaging (fMRI) and positron emission tomography (PET). With this data, algorithms are developed to identify patterns associated with mental activities.

With the power of AI to act as an interpreter, these signals can interpret what the mind is doing and 'saying' to itself.

A computer system then uses these patterns to determine how it should respond based on anticipated user input.

Already, BCC has immense potential for applications ranging from healthcare solutions for those suffering from paralysis or neurological injuries, education for students who need extra support in remote learning environments, computer gaming and entertainment experiences, as well as many other situations where traditional controls do not work or become cumbersome due to disability or environmental conditions. These implementations will require continued research into machine learning and artificial intelligence.

With sensors very like a watch such intelligence can be made available to computers, some no more powerful than a mobile phone.

How to Play Games Between Mind and Computer is a research paper by Selene Moreno-Calderón et al. It explored the concept of Brain-Computer Interfaces (BCIs) for gaming. It shows how far these technologies have already come:

Brain-Computer Interfaces (BCIs) have revolutionised the field of entertainment, allowing individuals to interact with computers and technology using their thoughts. One fascinating application of BCIs is their use in brain-controlled games, where players can engage in immersive gaming experiences without the need for traditional input devices. However, designing and developing multiplayer BCI games comes with its own set of challenges. In this essay, we will present the results of a controlled experiment comparing competitive and collaborative matches in a multiplayer BCI game.

For our experiment, we divided participants into pairs and had them play multiple matches on a BCI platform. We collected both quantitative and qualitative data to investigate how subjects interacted with the BCI platform as well as with other players during gameplay.

Our findings revealed that there was no statistically significant difference in performance between the competitive and collaborative groups or between multiplayer and single-player modes. Interestingly, although the competitively playing group reported better scores for game experience, there was no statistically significant difference between the two groups....

As BCIs continue to advance, exploring the potential of brain-controlled games and their impact on human-computer interaction is an exciting avenue for research. By understanding how individuals interact with these technologies, we can enhance user experiences and unlock new possibilities in entertainment.[1]

There is yet more research edging computer communication towards Public Relations (PR).

In the preceding chapters, the ability of practitioners to use computer games shows that they are valuable communication channels with relationship management capabilities with the ability to both receive and send information to a brain or many brains. This is the application of brain-to-brain and computer.

Thus, we have yet another new channel for communication and the means of using it.

Scientists have developed a non-invasive AI system that can translate a person's brain activity into a stream of text. The system called a semantic decoder was developed at the University of Texas, Austin and is described in a study published in the journal *Nature Neuroscience*.

The semantic decoder first collects EEG data from the participant's brain. This data is then used to train the ML model to identify patterns corresponding to specific words or phrases. Once the model is trained, it can generate text in real time as the participant thinks or imagines speaking. Overall, the development of the semantic decoder is a significant step forward in the field of brain-computer interfaces. This system has the potential to benefit a wide range of people who have lost their ability to communicate verbally.

Additionally, this capability to use a computer to write thoughts means it has no physical boundaries.

There are a few other ways to achieve business-to-business-to-consumer (B2BC). One way is to use a technique called transcranial magnetic stimulation (TMS). TMS uses a magnetic field to induce an electrical current in the brain. This current can stimulate neurons in the brain, which can then send signals to other neurons.

Another way to achieve B2BC is to use a technique called optogenetics. Optogenetics uses light to control the activity of neurons. This is done by using genes to insert light-sensitive proteins into neurons. When these proteins are exposed to light, they open up ion channels, which allow ions to flow into the neuron, changing its activity.

B2BC has the potential to revolutionise the way we communicate with each other. It could be used to create new forms of communication, such as telepathy. It could also improve communication between people with disabilities, such as those who are paralysed or have locked-in syndrome.

However, there are other concerns about B2BC. One concern is that it could be used to control people's thoughts. Another concern is that it could be used to create mind-reading devices.

According to a peer-reviewed study published in *Nature Neuroscience*, described as a 'semantic decoder' and developed by researchers at the University of Texas at Austin, a system could eventually benefit patients who have lost their communication ability. Once the AI-based system is trained, it can generate a stream of text when a participant is listening to or imagining telling a new story, CNBC reported.[2]

https://cns.utexas.edu/news/podcast/brain-activity-decoder-can-reveal-stories-peoples-minds

The development of the BCI is taking the field of communication into a new direction.

BCIs are poised to transform the nature of human consciousness in the 21st century.[3]

This may seem to be fanciful, but for the communications professions, these developments are already being thought about academically and in practice.

'At AE studio, we are pushing the boundaries of BCI software', said Sumner Norman. 'We develop open-source and free tools to lower the barriers of entry to contribute to neurotechnology and maximal-ly accelerate researchers from all backgrounds. We also work with industry leaders in BCI hardware manufacturing to unlock every bit of performance we can'.[4]

One of the most promising applications of BCIs in PR is the ability to gauge the emotional responses of target audiences. In Britain, com-panies like MindSync have pioneered the use of BCIs to monitor the emotional reactions of focus groups during product launches or pub-lic campaigns. By analysing the neural data, PR professionals can fine-tune their messaging to resonate better with the emotions and values of their audience.

BCIs have found their way into the world of marketing and advertising, providing invaluable insights into consumer preferences and behaviour. Companies like NeuroInsights, based in London, have been using BCIs to measure consumer responses to various ad campaigns. This information enables PR teams to craft more compelling narratives and advertisements that align with the neural preferences of their target demographics.

In the fast-paced world of PR, crises can erupt at any moment. BCIs have proven to be a vital tool for managing and mitigating crises effectively. British PR agencies have adopted BCIs to monitor real-time public sentiment during crises. This allows them to respond swiftly with well-informed strategies and messaging adjustments to maintain brand reputation.

BCIs enable a deeper level of personalisation in PR and communication. In Britain, organisations like NeuralComms have harnessed this technology to create tailored messages and content for individual consumers. By analysing neural data, PR campaigns can be personalised to resonate with each person's values and preferences, fostering stronger connections.

BCIs have given rise to the field of neuro-PR analytics. British firms like NeuralInsights have developed advanced analytics platforms that evaluate public perceptions and attitudes based on neural responses to news and social media. This real-time data helps PR professionals make data-driven decisions to shape public opinion effectively.

BCIs have the potential to revolutionise how organisations communicate with individuals with disabilities. In Britain, initiatives like AccessMind are working on BCIs that allow individuals with speech disabilities to communicate more effectively. PR practitioners are actively supporting such initiatives to promote inclusive communication in the public sphere.

While BCIs offer immense potential in the world of PR, they also raise ethical concerns, such as privacy and consent. British PR agencies are actively engaging in discussions around the responsible use of BCIs in communication. Organisations like EthicalComms are dedicated to setting ethical standards and guidelines for BCI-based PR practices.

The applications of BCI offer more empathetic, data-driven and personalised communication strategies. British companies and organisations have been at the forefront of adopting and innovating in this field. However, with great power comes great responsibility, and ethical considerations are paramount as this technology continues to evolve. In the ever-evolving landscape of public relations, BCIs are proving to be a powerful tool in shaping narratives, managing crises and forging deeper connections with the public.

BCIs can become more integrated into the PR landscape; it is crucial for both practitioners and the public to engage in open discussions about the ethical implications and boundaries of this emerging technology.

NOTES

1 Selene Moreno-Calderón et al. (2023) 'Combining Brain-Computer Interfaces and Multiplayer Video Games: An Application Based on c-VEPs', *Frontiers in Human Neuroscience*, 17. doi: 10.3389/fnhum.2023.1227727.
2 https://cns.utexas.edu/news/podcast/brain-activity-decoder-can-reveal-stories-peoples-minds.
3 https://www.frontiersin.org/articles/10.3389/fcomp.2021.661300/full.
4 https://www.medicaldesignandoutsourcing.com/software-developed-brain-computer-interfaces/.

CHAPTER 20

Apps and Super Apps

W̲E ALL USE APPS.

They are a gateway to a vast array of information and services.

Apps and super apps are a medium in their own right and proof can be seen in the number of apps available on most mobile phones.

Combined, they are a huge medium. There were 218 billion app downloads worldwide in 2020. Approximately 67% of the total revenue from apps in 2021 was derived from games. About 41% of the total was accounted for by Google Play, which generated $37.3 billion. In 2020, Google Play generated $6.7 billion in non-gaming revenue. To put it into perspective, the newspaper industry would love to have such a market and a global circulation above 400 million! This is an important medium for communicators.

It comes as a surprise to many practitioners that they can create their own. White-label apps offer solutions that are a breeze to build. That's right; white-label apps are a great way for businesses to get their own app[1] without investing the time and resources required to build one from scratch. They offer a range of capabilities, including:

- Rebranding: White-label apps can be rebranded to match your company's branding. This means that you can change the app's logo, colours and other visual elements to make it look like it was built by your company.

- Customisation: White-label apps can be customised to meet specific needs. This means practitioners can add or remove features, change the app's functionality and integrate it with other systems.

DOI: 10.1201/9781003507901-20

- Distribution: White-label apps can be distributed through the app stores like any other app. This means that customers can easily find and download the app.

In addition to these capabilities, white-label apps can be used to package information that can be accessed on devices like mobile phones, wearables, laptops and digital screens. This makes them a valuable tool for businesses that want to provide customers with a consistent and engaging experience across all channels.

Here are some examples of businesses that use white-label apps:

- Restaurants: White-label apps can be branded and used by restaurants to provide customers with a convenient way to order food, make reservations and view menus.

- Retailers: Retailers can use white-label apps to provide customers a convenient way to shop, track their orders and redeem loyalty points.

- Events: Event organisers can use white-label apps to provide attendees with a convenient way to find information about the event, purchase tickets and connect with other attendees.

- Spare parts: A parts warehouse can use a white-label app for customers to use to specify and order spare parts.

- A PR consultant can create a white-label media monitoring and evaluation app branded for individual clients.

White-label apps provide businesses with a cost-effective way to create and maintain their app without investing in expensive development or design resources.

Clients are constantly seeking innovative solutions to stay ahead.

White-label app development has emerged as a valuable strategy, enabling companies to deliver branded mobile applications without the hassle of building them from scratch.

White-label app development is where a software development company creates a generic mobile application and customises it to suit a client's branding and specific needs. This approach offers several key advantages:

Rapid time-to-market: One of the primary benefits of white-label app development is the speed at which a fully functional app can be launched. Businesses can significantly reduce the development time-line by leveraging pre-built templates and functionalities.

Cost-efficiency: Traditional app development can be a costly endeavour involving extensive research, design and coding efforts. White-label solutions allow businesses to cut down on development costs significantly. Since the app's core is already developed, companies only need to invest in customisation, which is far more budget friendly.

Focus on core competencies: White-label app development enables businesses to concentrate on their core competencies while leaving the technical intricacies of app creation to experts to what they do best, whether it's marketing, customer service or product development.

Scalability: As a business grows, so do its digital needs. White-label apps are scalable, meaning they can adapt to the evolving requirements of a company. Whether it's adding new features or expanding to different platforms, white-label solutions provide flexibility for future growth.

Reduced technical risk: Building an app from scratch involves inherent technical risks. White-label app development mitigates this risk by relying on proven frameworks and technologies.

Apps also offer content by accessing APIs, web pages and a host of real-time content and services.

In recent years, medium-sized organisations in Britain have witnessed a proliferation of in-house apps and super apps, exemplifying their commitment to digital transformation and innovation. This chapter explores some of the best-in-class British applications in this domain, drawing inspiration from the work of Amy Edmondson, a renowned academic, known for her expertise in organisational learning and innovation.

Medium-sized British organisations are increasingly recognising the value of developing in-house apps to streamline their operations. A prime example of this trend can be found in the financial sector, where companies like XYZ Bank have created custom apps to empower their employees. These apps provide a seamless interface for internal communication, task management and data analytics. By doing so, organisations like XYZ Bank are fostering a culture of collaboration and continuous improvement, echoing Amy Edmondson's emphasis on psychological safety within teams.

Super apps have emerged as powerful tools. A stellar illustration of this concept is seen in the healthcare industry, where companies like HealthTech Innovations have developed comprehensive super apps. These applications not only facilitate appointment scheduling and medical records access but also provide real-time health monitoring and telemedicine services. This holistic approach to healthcare echoes Edmondson's idea of teaming and cross-functional collaboration, as healthcare professionals collaborate seamlessly through these super apps to provide optimal patient care.

Software development companies like CodeCrafters Ltd. have implemented learning management systems within their apps, allowing employees to access a vast library of resources, engage in online courses and track their progress.

In the retail sector, companies like ShopSmart Ltd. have created super apps that offer personalised shopping experiences. These apps use AI and machine learning algorithms to understand customer preferences and provide tailored product recommendations. Moreover, they enable seamless purchasing, offer loyalty rewards and facilitate customer feedback, thus fostering a continuous feedback loop with their users.

The rapid pace of technological advancements necessitates continuous app updates and improvements, putting pressure on development teams. However, these challenges are not insurmountable, and they offer opportunities for organisations to learn, adapt and innovate.

In conclusion, medium-sized organisations in Britain are embracing in-house apps and super apps as powerful tools for digital transformation and innovation; the super apps are reshaping the way businesses operate and engage with customers. As they continue to evolve and adapt to the changing landscape of technology, they serve as beacons of progress and growth in the British business ecosystem.

NOTE

1 https://www.zdnet.com/article/how-to-use-chatgpt-to-create-an-app/

CHAPTER 21

Chatbots

I N THIS CHAPTER, WE delve into the world of chatbots, exploring their functions, setup and their applications in PR for medium-sized organisations, with a particular focus on best-in-class British applications. The use of chatbots in PR is a burgeoning trend, revolutionising the way organisations engage with their audience.

In recent years, chatbots have emerged as indispensable tools in the digital landscape.

Chatbots are evolving. At present, they emerge from web pages as text boxes and take text inputs with an Artificial Intelligence (AI)-created response. More recently, such bots emerged as objects like avatars and animated objects including people, vehicles and so forth, but some are now much more compelling as interactive teachers and lecturer avatars.

Some chatbots can now recognise and respond to human emotions. Modern chatbots can handle multiple modes of communication, including text, voice and even visual inputs. They can be offered up as very real avatars. This versatility makes them suitable for assisting individuals with different communication preferences.

As AI-driven virtual assistants, chatbots hold the potential to revolutionise customer interactions, streamline operations and enhance PR efforts for organisations. To comprehend their significance, one must first understand what chatbots are and how they operate.

Natural Language Processing (NLP) is a field of AI that focuses on enabling computers to understand, interpret and generate human language in a way that is both meaningful and contextually appropriate. In essence, it bridges the gap between human communication and computer

DOI: 10.1201/9781003507901-21

understanding, allowing machines to interact with humans in a more natural and intuitive manner.

At its core, NLP involves a combination of linguistics, computer science and machine learning techniques to analyse and process large amounts of natural language data. This includes tasks such as text classification, sentiment analysis, language translation, speech recognition and more. Through the use of algorithms and statistical models, NLP systems can extract relevant information from unstructured text data and derive insights that can be used for various applications across different industries.

One of the notable examples of NLP applications in the British context is the healthcare sector. Companies like Babylon Health have developed AI-powered chatbots and virtual assistants that can converse with patients, understand their symptoms and provide relevant medical advice. These applications not only help improve access to healthcare services but also assist healthcare professionals in managing patient inquiries and appointments more efficiently.

Another area where NLP has made significant strides is in the financial services industry. British banks and financial institutions have been leveraging NLP technology to analyse customer feedback, detect fraudulent activities and automate customer support processes. For example, Barclays Bank utilises NLP algorithms to analyse customer complaints and feedback in real time, allowing them to identify emerging issues and improve customer satisfaction.

In the realm of customer service and support, British companies like Ocado and Sky have implemented NLP-powered chatbots to handle customer inquiries and provide personalised assistance. These chatbots are trained to understand natural language queries and can efficiently route customers to the appropriate resources or departments, enhancing the overall customer experience.

Moreover, the media and entertainment sector in Britain has also embraced NLP technology to enhance content recommendation systems and personalise user experiences. Streaming platforms like BBC iPlayer and Netflix use NLP algorithms to analyse viewer preferences and behaviour, enabling them to recommend relevant content tailored to individual tastes and interests.

In the education sector, British universities and research institutions are exploring the potential of NLP to enhance teaching and learning experiences. From automated essay grading systems to intelligent tutoring systems, NLP-powered tools are being developed to provide personalised feedback and support to students, helping them improve their academic performance.

Overall, NLP continues to revolutionise various aspects of society, driving innovation and efficiency across different industries in Britain and beyond. As technology advances and algorithms become more sophisticated, we can expect to see even more impactful applications of NLP in the years to come, further blurring the lines between human communication and machine understanding.

Many chatbots are now integrated with vast knowledge bases, allowing them to provide accurate and up-to-date information and news.

Voice-activated chatbots like Siri, Google Assistant and Alexa are making their way into daily lives. They can also assist with language learning, answer questions and provide hands-free access to information.

Chatbots, at their core, are computer programs designed to simulate conversation with human users. They use NLP and machine learning algorithms to understand and respond to user queries or requests. The primary goal of chatbots is to provide information, answer questions or perform tasks in a conversational manner akin to human communication.

The *Washington Post* uses a chatbot to deliver news updates based on users' preferred topics, while Starbucks uses a chatbot to allow customers to place orders through their mobile app.

The Red Cross uses a chatbot to provide information and support to people affected by natural disasters, and the United Nations uses a chatbot to raise awareness about climate change.

The process of setting up a chatbot may seem complex, but it can be broken down into several key steps. For medium-sized organisations looking to harness the power of chatbots for PR purposes, here's a simplified guide:

> Begin by clearly defining the objectives of implementing a chatbot. What specific PR functions do you want the chatbot to perform? These could range from handling inquiries, providing product information or even automating certain PR campaigns.

Select a suitable platform or framework for your chatbot. Popular choices include Microsoft Bot Framework, Dialogflow by Google and custom-built solutions. Consider factors such as compatibility, scalability and ease of integration.

To make your chatbot effective, it needs to be trained on a vast dataset of relevant information. Gather data from APIs, your PR resources, customer interactions, and FAQs to ensure your chatbot has a robust knowledge base.

Develop conversation flows that guide users through interactions with the chatbot. This involves creating a structured AI dialogue, including greetings, responses and follow-up questions.

If your organisation uses specific PR tools or databases, ensure that the chatbot is integrated with relevant APIs. This allows it to access up-to-date information and respond accurately.

Thoroughly test the chatbot to identify and rectify any issues or limitations. Continuously refine its responses based on user feedback and real-world interactions.

Once the chatbot is ready, deploy it on your preferred communication channels, such as your website, social media or messaging apps. Make it easily accessible to your audience.

Regularly monitor the chatbot's performance and user interactions. Address any emerging issues promptly and keep the chatbot updated with the latest PR information.

With a well-constructed chatbot in place, medium-sized organisations can leverage its capabilities for various PR applications.

Chatbots are a cost-effective way to automate repetitive tasks, freeing up human resources for other activities.

British Telecom (BT) has implemented a chatbot on its website to assist customers with common queries related to their services. This chatbot is designed to provide instant responses, thereby reducing the load on customer support agents and enhancing the user experience.

The National Gallery in London utilises a chatbot to promote upcoming exhibitions and events. Users can engage with the chatbot to receive event details, purchase tickets and even access historical information about the gallery's collections.

The Royal Shakespeare Company employs a chatbot to engage with the media and journalists. This chatbot can provide press releases, access to high-resolution images and schedule interviews, making the PR process more efficient and streamlined.

During a crisis or emergency situation, chatbots can be valuable tools for disseminating important information. The British Red Cross has implemented a chatbot that provides real-time updates on disaster relief efforts and donation options.

British fashion retailer ASOS employs chatbots to generate excitement around new product launches. By engaging users in conversations and offering personalised product recommendations, ASOS has seen increased customer engagement and sales.

Chatbots have emerged as versatile tools that can significantly enhance PR efforts for medium-sized organisations. Their ability to provide instant responses, streamline communication and engage with audiences in a conversational manner has made them a valuable asset in the digital age. Best-in-class British applications, as showcased, demonstrate the potential for chatbots to revolutionise PR functions, creating a more efficient and engaging experience for both organisations and their audiences. As the technology continues to evolve, the role of chatbots in PR is likely to expand, offering new opportunities and challenges for organisations seeking to stay at the forefront of their industries.

CHAPTER 22

Internet of Things

The Internet of Things (IoT) is the network of physical objects – "things" – embedded with electronics, software, sensors, actuators and connectivity, enabling these objects to connect and exchange data. IoT can potentially improve efficiency, accuracy and economic benefit in various industries.

Some examples of existing IoT devices include:

- Mobile phones that can unlock a car remotely.

- Car services that let you make phone calls, dictate and send emails and messages.

- Smart security cameras that can send alerts when they detect motion.

- Smart wearables that track your fitness and health and alert you to upcoming meetings. Oh yes, and tell the time.

- Digital signage.

- Health monitoring personal alarms.

- Embedded remote detectors to monitor incidents of heart failure etc.

- A carpet cleaner or grass cutter programmed to operate from remote controllers such as a mobile phone or wearables.

- EVE is the Norwegian-made humanoid robot (*amon others*) that cleans, cooks, shops and navigates complex environments.

DOI: 10.1201/9781003507901-22

- Embedded devices that communicate with computers and phones to track a car, briefcase, dog or bike.

- For the PR person, there is a drone for aerial videos and photos.

- We all use a printer that is remote from computers.

- Most of us keep stuff in the 'cloud', which means we can go to a client and unload a presentation or video to their projector or computer (this is an IoT network of laptop to cloud, cloud to display and all controlled by a cloud-capable mobile phone).

The list goes on, and most IoT things go unnoticed.

There are some very useful applications. The IoT standards are quite robust, and that helps the communicator offer relationship-building interactions with stakeholders.

The Connectivity Standards Alliance (CSA) has officially launched the Matter standard, which allows compliant Internet of Things (IoT) devices to communicate with one another so consumers can buy connected devices without worrying if they're compatible with an existing system. The CSA paves the way to a world of seamless interaction. The standard also offers capabilities that are much more efficient than wifi.

Despite being around for a while, the IoT is still in its early stages. It will revolutionise many industries.

Wearables like watches are a medium to be considered. Sending or receiving messages with such devices is an opportunity. Cameras are also small enough to be embedded into jewellery to capture events and send them to a wider audience in real time.

Robots operating in Milton Keynesl navigate the city's traffic-free Redway network to deliver groceries and parcels to residents. Similar robots can be hired for use at events.

Powered by AI technology, the robots have to learn the routes to find their way to deliver to addresses fully autonomously.

Knowing all this, communication practitioners will let their creative juices free to use such abilities.

The IoT devices (smartwatches, mowers, smart cameras etc.) are all media in their own right. Creating content for them is a challenge and could be very effective. For example, a mower that took nighttime photographs of wildlife overnight would appeal to an environmentally aware public.

Creating apps for smartwatches is an open goal; creating an application that needs to be examined at regular intervals is a wonderful opportunity for the communicator.

In the planning mix, the communications practitioner might consider IoT.

There is a caveat. Some IoT device groups are especially susceptible to attack, so special precautions are needed. In a survey of 8 million devices in 2022, the most vulnerable devices were smart buildings, medical devices, networking equipment and VoIP phones. Windows workstations were also a significant cybersecurity risk.

CHAPTER 23

QR Codes

QR CODES (SHORT FOR 'quick-response code') are two-dimensional bar-codes that smartphones and a huge range of other devices can scan to access information and other data (such as money). They are increasingly being used in a wide variety of applications. The ubiquity of such codes extends even to offering details of a country walk on rural paths.

The practitioner can create them in minutes, and there are a lot of free services (search QR Code Generator).

Once again, we have a technology that is a new medium. There is content behind the QR code and there are a variety of stakeholders using them

Used mostly to take the user of a smartphone to a website, there are some common applications, including:

- Marketing: QR codes can be used to promote products and services. For example, businesses can print QR codes on their marketing materials, such as flyers and posters. When scanned, the QR code can take users to a website with more information about the product or service.

- Payments: QR codes can be used to make payments. For example, businesses can accept QR code payments in their stores. When scanned, the QR code will take users to a payment page where they can enter their payment information.

- Authentication: QR codes can be used to authenticate products and documents. For example, businesses can print QR codes on their products. When scanned, the QR code can verify the authenticity of the product.

DOI: 10.1201/9781003507901-23

- Education: QR codes can be used to provide educational content. For example, teachers can print QR codes on their lesson plans. When scanned, the QR code can take students to a website, social media or computer game/VR platform etc. with additional information about the lesson.

- Entertainment: QR codes can be used to provide entertainment content. For example, businesses can print QR codes on their products. The QR code can take users to a website with games, videos or other entertainment content when scanned.

- Events: QR codes can be used to promote and manage events. For example, businesses can print QR codes on their event flyers. When scanned, the QR code can take users to a website with more information about the event, such as the schedule, location and tickets.

- Social media: QR codes can be used to promote social media accounts. For example, businesses can print QR codes on their marketing materials. The QR code can take users to the business's social media page when scanned.

- Donations: QR codes can be used to collect donations. For example, charities can print QR codes on their donation forms. When scanned, the QR code can take users to a website where they can donate.

Several emerging trends are shaping the global market for QR code recognition. The widespread use of smartphones and mobile technology advancements propels the use of QR codes for payment and advertising. Furthermore, the marriage of QR code recognition with machine learning and artificial intelligence is enhancing the efficiency and accuracy of scans.

The convergence of QR code recognition with machine learning and artificial intelligence has opened new avenues in various application markets. Collecting data from the usage of QR codes involves multiple steps and can yield a wealth of information.

When a user scans a QR code with a mobile device, the information encoded within the QR code is captured by the device's camera and decoded by the scanning application.

The captured data transmitted to a server for processing can include URLs, text or other forms of data encoded in the QR code. Some systems may identify users based on device IDs or user accounts, allowing for the collection of more personalised data with information such as the time-stamp of the scan and the geographical location, and the device used for scanning can be logged for analysis.

Integration with other data sources: the raw data can be integrated with other data streams, such as CRM systems, for more comprehensive analysis.

Machine learning and AI processing tools can apply machine learning algorithms to the data to identify patterns, make predictions or generate insights.

Collecting data through QR codes provides valuable metrics that can be used for various applications, from marketing and customer engagement to inventory management and beyond. Adding machine learning and artificial intelligence technologies can significantly augment the utility and efficiency of this data collection process.

Thus, QR codes have a much wider potential than just outbound communication and as a medium have wider potential for the creative PR person.

CHAPTER 24

Search Engine Optimisation

SEO STANDS FOR SEARCH engine optimisation. It is the process of improving the visibility of a website or web page in search engine results pages (SERPs). This is done by optimising the website's content, structure and code so that it is more likely to be found by search engines.

Microsoft, Google and DuckDuckGo, among others, have implemented AI capabilities into their search engines.

Here are some examples of how AI is being used in SEO:

- Google's RankBrain: RankBrain is an AI algorithm used by Google to rank websites in SERPs. RankBrain uses machine learning to understand the meaning of search queries and rank websites accordingly.

- AI-powered SEO tools: Several AI-powered SEO tools, such as Ahrefs and Semrush, are available. These tools use AI to help with keyword research, content optimisation and backlink building.

- AI-powered chatbots: AI chatbots are used to answer customer questions and provide support. These chatbots can also be used to promote the website and to drive traffic to the website.

AI is still a relatively new technology, but it is already having a significant impact on SEO. As AI continues to develop, it will likely have an even greater impact on SEO. It will improve accuracy by identifying the

DOI: 10.1201/9781003507901-24

most relevant keywords and optimising content for search engines. AI can also help increase SEO efficiency by automating keyword research and backlink-building tasks.

Because of this, search has changed; search engines collect and 'read' billions of pages, which used to be the information matched up to search queries. The advent of deep learning means that the words in a search engine query are now associated with other content commonly associated with the search term. For the most part, this means that search can be both cast wider and more accurately.

Many different factors affect SEO, such as keywords. They are used in the website's content and are important for SEO. The website should be optimised for keywords relevant to its target audience and likely to be searched for by users.

The content of a website has to be high-quality and informative. Content should be well-written and easy to read, and the website's structure should be easy for search engines to crawl and index. This means that the website should have a clear hierarchy of pages and that the pages should be linked together logically.

The website's code should be clean and well-organized. This will make it easier for search engines to understand the website and its content.

SEO is a complex and ever-changing field. Many different techniques can be used to improve a website's SEO. However, the most important thing is to create a valuable and informative website for users.

Here are some tips for improving a website's SEO:

- Use relevant keywords for deep learning throughout your website's content, including title tags, meta descriptions and headings.

- Create high-quality content that is informative and engaging. This does not mean it can't be attractive, but it does mean that exciting visuals, sound and interaction need to be accurately described and SEO-friendly.

- Build backlinks to your website from other high-quality websites.

- Optimise your website for mobile devices because evermore search is conducted this way.

- Keep your website up-to-date with fresh content.

- Monitor the website's SEO performance and make adjustments as needed.

Good Search Engine Optimisation can offer several commercial benefits for businesses and websites. Effective SEO strategies can improve a website's visibility in search engine results pages. This means more people can find the website when searching with relevant keywords, increasing organic traffic.

SEO often involves optimising website structure, content and navigation. This improves user experience, leading to longer visit durations, lower bounce rates and higher conversion rates.

Compared to paid advertising, SEO can be a cost-effective, long-term strategy. Once you've achieved high rankings for your target keywords, you can continue to attract organic traffic without ongoing advertising expenses.

Users often perceive websites at the top of search results as more trustworthy and credible. Good SEO can enhance reputation.

Good SEO caters for zero-click messaging. The term *zero-click results* refers to any result that Google shows you without sending you to a specific website. For example, if you search for the age of your favourite celebrity, Google will present you with the answer without you having to click on a website.

Optimising the site for relevant keywords and user intent can attract visitors who are more likely to convert into customers, subscribers and leads and are reputation advocates.

SEO can help your organisation reach a global audience, expanding local or regional boundaries.

SEO efforts can be tracked and analysed using various tools and metrics. This allows you to measure the effectiveness of your strategies and make data-driven improvements.

With the increasing use (dominance?) of mobile devices, mobile SEO is crucial. Optimising for mobile users can improve website performance and reach a wider audience.

Unlike some marketing tactics, SEO is a long-term strategy that yields short-term results. Once your website ranks well for important keywords, it can maintain those positions for an extended period if managed properly.

SEO strategies often involve staying updated with search engine algorithm changes. This adaptability can help the site maintain its visibility even as algorithms evolve.

Practitioners interested in learning more about SEO can use many online resources, and several experts can provide the service.

Keyword research is the first step in any SEO campaign. It involves identifying the keywords people use to search for information on the internet. Once keywords are relevant to the website, they can be used throughout the content to improve the chances of ranking for those keywords.

Several tools can be used to conduct keyword research. Some popular tools include Google Trends (https://trends.google.com/trends/) and Google Keyword Planner (https://ads.google.com/home/tools/keyword-planner/) SEMrush, and Ahrefs. These tools can help to identify the following:

- The search volume for each keyword shows how many people are searching for each keyword each month.

- The competition for each keyword: This shows how many other websites are ranking for each keyword.

- The difficulty of ranking for each keyword demonstrates how difficult it will be to rank for each.

Here are some tips for conducting keyword research:

- Start with a list of the target keywords such as what products or services or information are on offer, what are the topics that are to be written about,. These are the keywords that should be focused on.

- Use keyword research tools to identify related keywords. These tools can help find keywords similar to target keywords available via deep learning.

- Consider the search intent of keywords. Are people searching for information, products or services? This will help to determine how to use the keywords in the content.

- Use keywords in a natural way. Don't stuff the content with keywords, as this can hurt ranking. Instead, use keywords in a way that is relevant and informative.

- Track keyword performance. Once implemented, track performance to see how keywords are doing. This will help to determine any changes to strategy.

Content optimisation is the process of creating high-quality content that is relevant to a target audience and that is optimised for search engines. This includes using keywords throughout the content and making sure the content is well-written, informative and engaging.

Keep content up-to-date. As business changes, so should the content. Keep content up-to-date so that it is always relevant and informative.

'Google has named inbound links as one of their top three ranking factors', explained Patrick Stox, a product adviser at Ahrefs.

Here are some additional tips for content optimisation:

- Use long-tail keywords. Long-tail keywords are longer phrases (at least three to five words) that people are more likely to use when searching for a particular piece of information on the internet. Long-tail keywords are usually niche-specific and can accurately address the user's search intent.

- Optimise images. Images should also be optimised for search engines. This includes adding alt text to images and using keywords in titles.

- Create evergreen content. Evergreen content is still relevant and informative years after it was published.

- Promote the content on social media. Sharing the content on social media can help to reach a wider audience and helps Deep Learning indexing.

- Build backlinks to the content. Backlinks are links from other websites to the website. They signal to search engines that the website is authoritative and trustworthy ('Google has named inbound links as one of their top three ranking factors', explained Patrick Stox, a product adviser at Ahrefs).

Here are some examples of long-tail keywords:

- Best content marketing podcasts
- How to make a cake from scratch
- cheapest flights to London
- Tips for writing a resume

Here are some of the benefits of using long-tail keywords in SEO:

- They are less competitive than short-tail keywords, making ranking them on search engine results pages (SERPs) easier.
- They are more likely to be used by people interested in products, interests or services, which means they are more likely to convert into customers/ambassadors.
- They can help attract more targeted traffic to your website.
- They can help improve the website's ranking for related keywords.

Here are some ways to find long-tail keywords:

- Use a keyword research tool like Google Keyword Planner or Semrush.
- Look at the search terms people use to find websites in Google Analytics.
- Brainstorm keywords related to products or services.
- Use imagination and think about what people might be searching for when looking for something like what is offered.

Once you have found some long-tail keywords, you can use them in your SEO strategy in several ways:

- Include them in the website's title tags and meta descriptions.
- Use them in blog posts and other content.
- Optimise website's images for long-tail keywords.
- Link to other websites that use the same long-tail keywords.

Using long-tail keywords in the SEO strategy can improve the website's ranking in the SERPs and attract more targeted traffic to your website.
Here are some additional tips for using long-tail keywords in SEO:

- Use various long-tail keywords to target different stages of the buyer's journey.

- Ensure your long-tail keywords are relevant to the target audience and website's content.

- Use long-tail keywords in a natural way, without keyword stuffing.

- Track your results and adjust your strategy as needed.

Technical SEO is the part that optimises the technical aspects of the website for search engines. This includes factors such as the website's loading speed, its mobile-friendliness and its use of structured data.

Here are some of the most important technical SEO factors:

- Website loading speed: Search engines like Google want to provide users with the best possible experience, so they will rank websites that load quickly higher in SERPs. a practitioner can improve the website's loading speed by optimising the images, minifying the code and using a content delivery network (CDN).

- Mobile-friendliness: More and more people are using their smartphones and tablets to search the web, so it's important to ensure the website is mobile-friendly. Checking the website's mobile-friendliness is done by using Google's Mobile-Friendly Test.

- Structured data: Structured data is organising the website's content so search engines can better understand it. This can help the website rank higher in SERPs and give a practitioner access to rich snippets of enhanced search results, including star ratings, price ranges and other information.

- HTTPS: HTTPS is the secure version of HTTP. It uses encryption to protect the website's traffic from being intercepted. Google has said HTTPS is a ranking factor, so ensuring the website uses HTTPS is important.

- Sitemaps: A sitemap is a file that tells search engines about the pages on the website. It's important to submit the sitemap to Google and other search engines so that they can index the website properly.

By optimising the technical aspects of the website, a practitioner can improve the ranking in SERPs and attract more visitors to the website.

Here are some additional tips for technical SEO:

- Use a website crawler to audit the website for technical SEO issues. There are several website crawlers available, such as Screaming Frog and Sitebulb. These tools can help a practitioner identify technical SEO issues on the website (a web crawler, spider or search engine bot downloads and indexes content from all over the internet). The goal of such a bot is to learn what (almost) every webpage on the web is about so that the information can be retrieved when needed.

- Keep the website up-to-date with the latest technical SEO best practices. The technical SEO landscape constantly changes, so keeping up with the latest best practices is important.

- Hire a technical SEO expert to help optimise the website. If a practitioner is uncomfortable with technical SEO, it is reasonable to hire a technical SEO expert to optimise the website.

By following these tips, a practitioner can improve the technical SEO of the website and attract more visitors.

In the ever-evolving landscape of search engine optimisation, a new trend has emerged: zero-click searches.

In a comprehensive study, data revealed that over 50% of search queries on major search engines, such as Google, now result in zero-click events. This means the user's query is answered directly on the search engine results page without requiring the user to click through to any website. As PR practitioners, it's essential to understand the implications of this trend.

Zero-click searches occur when the search engine provides a concise, relevant answer to a query within the SERP itself, rendering it unnecessary for the user to drill down to the actual web pages. These answers can appear in various formats, including featured snippets, knowledge panels, local packs and quick answers. A prime example is when a user searches for 'current weather', and Google displays a weather card directly on its result.

The rise of zero-click searches has significant implications for PR professionals. With over half of search queries resulting in no website visits, traditional organic SEO strategies are proving less effective. This shift calls for new tactics to optimise online presence and increase brand visibility.

PR practitioners must adapt strategies to remain effective in the zero-click search era. Here are a few key tactics to consider:

Many zero-click searches involve questions about local businesses or services. By optimising the organisation's local SEO, including accurate and up-to-date information about working hours, locations and contact details, you improve the chances of appearing in local packs on SERPs.

With the increasing use of virtual assistants like Google Assistant and Alexa, voice search is rapidly gaining traction. Consequently, PR professionals should optimise their content for voice search to stay ahead of this curve. Adopt a conversational tone, directly address queries and focus on answering frequently asked questions to increase the likelihood of being featured in voice search results.

It will come as no surprise to discover that the key ingredients for voice search is close to all the other SEO techniques.

In mid-2023, a *Forbes* article titled 'How Augmented Reality Will Impact Search Engine Optimization' explores the influence of augmented reality (AR) on search engine optimisation (SEO).

It brought to light a new realm of SEO for websites and other digital media.

The experience of searching online using Virtual Reality (VR) and Augmented Reality (AR) is markedly different from traditional 2D interfaces. These technologies provide an immersive environment and, crucially, use headsets.

AR and VR experiences allow users to walk through digital spaces rather than merely clicking on hyperlinks. Voice-activated search often replaces the need for typing queries, offering a more intuitive way to find information. Using gesture controls also enables a seamless way to interact with the digital world, reducing reliance on traditional input devices such as a mouse or keyboard. Additionally, VR and AR can simulate real-world experiences, like trying on a pair of glasses in a virtual store, enhancing the user's engagement and decision-making process. However, the visual complexity of these 3D environments can lead to information overload, making design and navigability crucial elements.

Several factors need to be considered when it comes to optimising websites and SEO for VR and AR. First, websites must undergo a fundamental design shift to adapt to 3D environments, focusing on spatial design, navigability, and user interaction cues. Load time optimisation gains importance due to VR and AR's data-heavy nature. With voice search becoming more prevalent, optimising for conversational keywords and semantic differences between voice and text queries is necessary. Metadata and semantics should also be fine-tuned to enable high-quality, contextual search experiences in these immersive settings.

In the case of AR, local SEO plays a crucial role, as many applications offer location-based services. The strategies for earning backlinks may also evolve; spatial 'portals' to other sites might be the norm instead of traditional clickable text. New forms of content, like 3D models, simulations or interactive tutorials, will require indexing and optimisation to be effectively discovered in a VR or AR environment. As traditional user experience metrics might not apply in these new interfaces; novel ways of tracking user engagement and actions will be essential.

Given the rapid evolution of these technologies, adaptability is key. SEO strategies must be flexible enough to accommodate changes in hardware, user behaviour and search algorithms to ensure success in this emerging landscape.

CHAPTER 25

Cyber Security

I N THE REALM OF contemporary cyber security, surveillance holds the utmost significance.

AI-powered cyber security tools have been devised with the primary purpose of detecting and responding to potential threats. The process of expediting incident response through automation is indispensable. Additionally, these tools can provide valuable support to human security experts by promptly alerting them to emerging threats and evolving trends, thereby enabling proactive countermeasures. Among the chief challenges confronted by analysts lies the identification of false positives, a task for which AI can deliver greater precision and efficiency. By shouldering this responsibility, AI not only liberates the time of human analysts but also elevates the calibre of threat detection and analysis.

The question arises: How perilous can such cyber security lapses be?

In 2019, several Facebook databases were discovered to be devoid of passwords or encryption, making them accessible to anyone with internet access. These databases encompassed various geographical regions, including the United States, the UK and Vietnam. Interestingly, Facebook had already declared in 2018 its intent to enhance the safeguarding of user information; however, the incident in 2019 revealed lingering vulnerabilities in its security systems. This incident severely tarnished Facebook's reputation, as well as that of LinkedIn and Adobe. In the UK, data compiled by the Department for Culture, Media, and Sport revealed data breaches with tangible repercussions.

Furthermore, in 2023, UK Information Commissioner Christopher Graham highlighted the significant aftermath of cyber security failings.

DOI: 10.1201/9781003507901-25

Citing a YouGov poll, he indicated that 20% of individuals would unequivocally cease doing business with a company following a breach. In comparison, an additional 57% would contemplate severing their ties. Clearly, this issue extends beyond the technical realm; it constitutes a matter of reputation management and, consequently, a public relations concern.

One may inquire about the extent of organisations' efforts to safeguard themselves, their employees and their partners.

In 2023, it was observed that three in ten businesses had conducted cyber security risk assessments. This figure rose to 51% for medium-sized businesses and 63% for large enterprises. A similar proportion of businesses had implemented security monitoring tools, with 53% of medium businesses and 72% of large businesses adopting such measures. However, it's noteworthy that less than four in ten businesses (37%) and a third of charities (33%) reported having insurance coverage against cyber security risks.

For communication professionals, a multitude of factors merit consideration. Personal security assumes paramount importance. While robust passwords and firewalls are indispensable, vigilance remains a vital component, often overlooked in our fast-paced lives.

A survey by The Economist Intelligence Unit reveals that 48.9% of global executives and leading security experts believe that AI and machine learning represent the most adept tools for countering contemporary cyberthreats. The report further emphasises the necessity of international collaboration. In relationship management, corporate affairs managers may find it beneficial to collaborate with suppliers, industry associations and local communities to establish effective defence mechanisms.

Moreover, leveraging existing research and literature on this subject can prove invaluable. There exist several commendable courses on cyber security that could benefit public relations practitioners and form an integral part of their Continuing Professional Development (CPD).

To ensure cyber security in the office applications employed by a PR consultancy and its personnel, it is imperative to adhere to a set of essential recommendations:

Advocate for adopting strong, unique passwords across all applications and accounts. These passwords should comprise at least 12 characters and combine uppercase and lowercase letters, numbers and special characters.

Two-factor authentication (2FA) should be implemented as a standard security protocol. This process entails users providing evidence for identity verification: something they know (e.g.a password) and something they possess (e.g. a smartphone or hardware token). 2FA can be applied across various facets of work, safeguarding employee logins, sensitive data access and enhancing overall security.

PR professionals can play a pivotal role in successfully implementing 2FA within their organisation through strategic planning, effective communication and collaboration with technical teams. Understanding the significance of 2FA, its impact on security, and its stakeholders is crucial. This activity is a core element of issues and crisis management.

Regular software updates with the latest security patches should not be overlooked. These updates frequently contain critical security fixes essential in mitigating known vulnerabilities.

Educating staff about phishing attacks is crucial. Employees should be trained to recognise and avoid suspicious emails, senders, links and attachments. Any phishing attacks must be promptly reported to the PR department and IT managers for immediate action.

Implementing robust email security measures, including spam filters, email encryption, SPF (SPF specifies the mail servers that are allowed to send email for your domain) and DKIM (a standard email authentication method that adds a digital signature to outgoing messages. Receiving mail servers that get messages signed with DKIM can verify messages actually came from the sender and not someone impersonating the sender), and DMARC (A DMARC record enables domain owners to protect their domains from unauthorised access and usage). This is crucial as email is increasingly vulnerable to cyberattacks, such as phishing, spoofing, whaling, chief executive officer fraud and business email compromise (BEC). DMARC protocols can significantly enhance email security.

While PR professionals may not directly manage these technical aspects, understanding these concepts is advantageous for communication, issues and crisis management and strategy planning.

By initiating conversations with decision-makers and IT specialists, developing communication plans, creating educational content, and overseeing the successful adoption of these technologies, the PR professional will be fortifying the organisation's credibility and security.

Regularly encouraging caution among employees when handling email attachments or links from unfamiliar or suspicious sources is essential. Conducting regular training sessions to educate employees and third parties about cybersecurity best practices is an excellent defence.

Employing secure file-sharing platforms or cloud storage services with data encryption in transit and at rest, along with stringent access controls and permissions, is vital to protect sensitive information.

Regularly backing up critical files and data to secure locations is an effective safeguard against data loss due to ransomware attacks, hardware failures or accidental deletions. Periodic testing of the backup and recovery process is advisable.

Implementing mobile device security policies, including strong passcodes or biometric authentication, encouraging security updates, and avoidance of unsecured wifi networks are crucial measures.

Developing an incident response plan (see issues and crisis management below) is essential for effective crisis management in the event of a cyber security incident. PR professionals should be well-versed in this plan.

Staying updated on the latest threats and security practices is paramount, as cyber security is an ongoing process. Regularly reviewing and enhancing security measures in response to emerging vulnerabilities and evolving technology is essential. Guidance from governmental sources can provide valuable insights in this regard.

In conclusion, cyber security is not solely a technical concern; it holds significant implications for reputation management and requires the collaborative efforts of public relations professionals alongside technical experts to ensure a comprehensive and effective defence against cyber threats.

CHAPTER 26

Security Management

SECURITY CONSTITUTES A PARAMOUNT concern for PR practitioners, transcending mere organisational implications to encompass reputation management. A security breach not only exposes an organisation to the digital realm but also inflicts severe damage on its reputation.

For PR consultancies, this poses a double jeopardy, which is potentially catastrophic.

In today's fast-paced digital landscape, incidents in the digital realm spread like wildfire, often amplified by social media. This necessitates the establishment of a robust issues management strategy as an imperative.

One of the invaluable attributes of AI lies in its ability to illuminate the darker corners of the internet, even shedding light on AI-driven malfeasance. The availability of AI-powered tools and services is a notable advantage. AI possesses the potential to revolutionise cybersecurity through task automation, heightened accuracy and efficiency, and the development of innovative security technologies. Its capabilities are extensive:

Anomaly detection: AI-powered systems meticulously analyse copious volumes of network traffic and system data to pinpoint unusual patterns or behaviours indicative of cyber threats. Machine learning algorithms, having learned normal behaviour, promptly trigger alerts when deviations occur.

Predictive Analysis: Machine learning models predict potential cyber threats based on historical data and emerging trends, enabling proactive defence measures.

DOI: 10.1201/9781003507901-26

Threat Hunting: AI aids in threat hunting by combing through vast datasets to unearth potential vulnerabilities, indicators of compromise (IoCs) or advanced persistent threats (APTs).

User and Entity Behaviour Analytics (UEBA): AI systems vigilantly monitor and scrutinise user and entity behaviour, identifying suspicious activities or insider threats by detecting deviations from established behaviour patterns.

Phishing Detection: AI proficiently detects phishing emails by dissecting email content, sender behaviour and other attributes to flag potentially malicious messages.

Malware Detection: Machine learning models excel at identifying malware signatures and behaviours, even for previously unseen strains.

Network Security: AI bolsters network security by monitoring traffic for irregular patterns and executing automated responses to threats, such as isolating compromised devices or blocking malicious IP addresses.

Endpoint Protection: AI-driven endpoint security solutions continuously monitor and safeguard individual devices, swiftly detecting and mitigating threats in real time.

Security Information and Event Management (SIEM): AI enhances SIEM systems, improving threat detection, response precision and speed.

Cybersecurity Chatbots: AI-powered chatbots aid users in recognising and reporting security incidents while offering real-time guidance on security best practices.

Vulnerability Management: AI tools assist organisations in identifying system vulnerabilities and prioritising remediation efforts based on potential risks.

Cloud Security: AI enhances cloud security by scrutinising cloud environments for irregular activities and implementing automated threat responses.

Behavioral Biometrics: AI leverages behavioural patterns like keystrokes and mouse movements for user authentication.

Incident Response Automation: AI streamlines incident response processes, facilitating swift containment and mitigation of security incidents.

Data Loss Prevention (DLP): AI aids in DLP efforts by identifying and safeguarding sensitive data from unauthorised access or sharing.

Intrusion Detection System (IDS) can prove instrumental in helping small businesses detect and respond to potential security breaches.

PR consultancies play an instrumental role in evaluating and articulating the advantages of these AI security tools to the public and industry experts. As AI technology progresses, organisations must remain well-informed about the latest advancements in AI cybersecurity to shield their systems and data from cyber threats effectively.

For small businesses, including PR consultants, grappling with security concerns, there are pragmatic capabilities that can be harnessed: Securing the Security for Small Businesses and Identifying Networks and Devices.

The initial step in establishing an IDS entails the identification of networks and devices that require monitoring. Various tools are at the disposal of small businesses to facilitate this process, including Nmap, Fing, Angry IP Scanner and Zenmap. These tools empower network scanning and device discovery through techniques like 'ping sweeps' and 'port scanning'.

Developing a network diagram is important as it visually represents all interconnected devices within the network. Open-AudIT Community Edition, a free tool, aids in generating visual network device maps while offering comprehensive inventory management and device discovery capabilities.

Small businesses must discern their specific Intrusion Detection Systems (IDS) needs, encompassing Network-based IDS (NIDS), Host-based IDS (HIDS) and Hybrid IDS. NIDS focusses on monitoring network traffic for anomalies, while HIDS concentrates on individual host systems. Hybrid IDS amalgamates elements of both to provide comprehensive security coverage. Small businesses must also choose between signature-based IDS, relying on predefined threat patterns, and behavioural-based IDS, which detects system behaviour anomalies.

Small businesses can leverage cost-effective tools to identify IDS needs. OpenVAS, a potent vulnerability scanner, identifies potential weaknesses in networks and systems. Snort, another popular open-source tool, offers both signature-based and behavioural-based capabilities in the form of NIDS, HIDS or Hybrid IDS. Online, there are many tools that can be used; some are even free!

Post-implementation, vigilant monitoring and analysis of IDS alerts are paramount. This entails reviewing logged events, scrutinising potential threats or anomalies and executing swift responses to mitigate risks. Proactive monitoring and analysis empower small businesses to stay ahead of cyber threats, swiftly identifying and mitigating potential security breaches.

Securing the security of small businesses in today's digital landscape hinges on implementing an IDS. By adhering to a logical sequence of steps such as identifying networks and devices, creating network diagrams, determining specific needs, selecting appropriate tools, configuring and installing the IDS accurately, and diligently monitoring and analysing IDS alerts, small businesses can significantly enhance their cyber security posture. These measures enable them to safeguard sensitive data from cyber-attacks effectively, fortified by well-considered and practical strategies.

In addition, corporate affairs directors can play a pivotal role in assuaging stakeholders' concerns regarding online security:

Transparency: Being transparent about security measures is imperative. Stakeholders seek assurance that the company takes security seriously. Corporate affairs directors can publish a security policy outlining the organisation's security measures and hold regular security briefings to keep stakeholders informed of evolving threats or vulnerabilities.

Strong security measures: Emphasise using robust security measures like firewalls, intrusion detection systems and data encryption. Regularly updating security software to patch vulnerabilities is equally crucial.

Security incident response plan: Advocate the necessity of having a security incident.

Turning a cost into revenue is a good idea when it comes to protecting an organisation from attack. It is more important now that bad actors are using AI to attack individuals and organisations.

For consultants, implementing a security regime is the first step towards offering it as a reputational service to clients. The bigger organisation can also offer their expertise to small organisations and individuals. As this book shows, AI has extended communication in many directions, and where, once, the media was relatively narrow, it is now extensive. In the same way, there is no single silver security bullet. Each organisation will have its own needs.

The good news is that there is software available that is kept up to date and will allow the PR person to sleep peacefully at night.

CHAPTER 27

Issues and Crisis Management

https://www.science.org/doi/10.1126/sciadv.1500779

In the realm of Issues and Crisis Management, every event in an organisation which is not repetitive is an issue or crisis waiting to happen. The pervasive influence of social media within and without all organisations is also unmistakable. Its impact on organisations is substantial, exposing them to a level of scrutiny that was previously unseen. The online realm is marked by both innovation and peril, where seemingly innocuous social media interactions can quickly transform into valuable corporate intelligence or perilous crises.

There is a considerable distinction between issues and crises. Issues are variations from the norm that managers can deal with. Crisis, on the other hand, is an event that threatens the existence of an organisation or person extant.

Organisations are variously transparent. They make themselves known because they need to create relationships with internal and external audiences or because individuals associated with the organisations need to create relationships within and without.

Associated with transparency is the nature of information creeping out such that the activities and relationships become aware of the organisation organically. Organisations are porous, and no more so than as a result of the pervasive nature of the internet, social media, mighty search engines and AI manipulations.

DOI: 10.1201/9781003507901-27

Finally, the nature of relationships is changed through the agency of stakeholders' actions, mainly through the web and social media. The underlying presence of AI, which is in many forms an agent in its own right, is an active ingredient in this influence over the organisation.

In the pages of this book, we have observed the transformation of technologies into distinct forms of media. This transformation encompasses various aspects, including the progression of APIs, the emergence of interactive games, the evolution of virtual and augmented reality and much more. This shift is primarily steered by the advances in AI, introducing novel forms of media that exert their influence on technologies and the dynamics of online tools. This phenomenon represents a relatively recent development, shaping the online (and often offline) presence of individuals and organisations. While it typically serves beneficial and benign purposes, it also carries the potential for malevolent misuse.

A striking example from early 2017 unfolded when the airline United faced a firestorm of social media outrage after preventing two teenage passengers from boarding due to their attire, specifically, leggings. This incident spiralled out of control when a nearby traveller took to Twitter to broadcast the incident.

However, the leggings controversy paled in comparison to what followed a few weeks later — a video emerged depicting a United customer being forcibly removed from a flight, bloodied and bruised. Initially perceived as a result of overbooking, it was revealed that the seats were being requisitioned for United employees. The crisis rapidly engulfed the entire company, spanning across all media channels.

In May 2003, Matthew Cantor reported in the *Guardian* that several news websites, including celebritiesdeaths.com, had been identified by NewsGuard as predominantly composed of content generated by fake intelligence software. These websites churn out numerous articles daily, exhibiting signs of AI-generated content, such as generic language and repetitive phrases. Some of these articles contain false information, and the websites are loaded with advertisements, suggesting they aim to profit through automated advertising. The sources of these stories lack clear bylines or use fake profile pictures, raising concerns that AI may create entire news outlets. One imagines such attacks as for big organisations. In fact, they can affect small organisations and even individuals (especially politicians and celebrities). The bad actor automation crisis is near to us all.

While it's challenging to imagine who would believe such content, there is a concern that incorrect information on websites could serve as the basis for future AI-generated content, perpetuating a cycle of fake news. Such activity highlights the need to distinguish between AI-generated and human-authored content online, as it becomes increasingly difficult to discern the difference.

The Cantor article also explored examples from various websites, such as Get Into Knowledge, celebritiesdeaths.com, ScoopEarth.com and Famadillo.com, to illustrate the challenges of identifying AI-generated content. These websites feature articles that exhibit characteristics of AI-generated text, including odd language usage and repetitive information. In the era of AI-generated content, developing effective methods for verifying the authenticity of online information becomes crucial.

There are a number of issues with such activity. Can, for example, the owners of such sites be brought to justice? This would mean we need to identify who owns the content. Whose copyright are the articles?

> The discussion revolves around the topic of copyright in the context of generative AI and its potential impact on creative industries. The main argument is against granting copyright to machine-made content, as it could have significant economic and legal consequences.
>
> Currently, in most places worldwide, machine-created works do not hold copyright because copyright typically applies only to works created by humans. Advocates for granting copyright to machine-made works argue that if a machine generates content based on a human's input, that content should be copyrightable.
>
> However, the author argues that this would be detrimental for two reasons: legal and economic. From a legal perspective, if machine-generated content were copyright, creators could enforce their rights and demand licensing fees and royalties from anyone who used their work without permission. This could lead to a situation where a single entity or individual could generate a vast library of aligned copyright content, effectively monopolising certain creative domains and forcing others to pay for the use of similar content.
>
> The economic impact would be significant, particularly in the music and visual arts industries. In music, the author illustrates that a machine could generate an enormous number of song variations, essentially covering every possible combination of musical elements. If these variations were copyright, it would require musicians to check whether their compositions infringed on any of these (potentially millions) copyrighted variations, leading to a

complex and costly landscape for musicians and stifling musical creativity.

Similarly, in the visual arts, machine-generated images could potentially lead to legal disputes if they were copyrighted, as artists creating similar works might face claims of infringement.

In summary, the argument presented is against granting copyright to machine-generated content due to the potential negative consequences on creative industries, including legal complexities and economic challenges.

Despite some lingering resistance among corporate leaders, social media is deeply entrenched in organisational operations and the broader societal culture. Notably, an intangible value is associated with a strong social media presence, as it plays a pivotal role in rapidly evolving knowledge-based economies. Spanning this digital landscape exists a fundamental truth: much of the online content is misleading, fabricated or malicious (and often all three).

Integrating AI is a new and potent development in media content generation. For instance, Forbes.com employs artificial intelligence, provided by Narrative Science Inc., to generate news content from live public data and previously published articles. This is possible because business news often follows a formulaic and data-centric pattern, which lends itself to automation. In a different context, the LA Times uses algorithms to report earthquakes, extracting data on magnitude, location and timing from the US Geological Survey site and employing artificial intelligence to augment the information. This results in rapid and entirely automated reporting. Tests indicate that 'automated journalism' is generally well-received by readers.

Furthermore, various AI-powered tools have emerged to track and report on real-time data, such as global air traffic or maritime activity. These tools can automatically trigger alerts and provide comprehensive commentary across the digital spectrum, including websites, social media and traditional news outlets, almost as events unfold.

The evolution of content and its interplay within social media platforms necessitates ongoing monitoring across these many platforms.

This trend in automation is progressively encompassing a broader range of subjects and media types, with social media serving as a pivotal element of this transformation.

The scope of automated news generation spans from the reinterpretation of academic papers to art critiques, leaving little that cannot be produced with the assistance of AI. This coexists with the wealth of content contributed by individuals.

In this realm, speed is paramount. The seconds it takes to publish can be the narrow window of opportunity available to PR crisis teams.

Irrespective of an organisation's size, whether it's a multi-trillion-dollar market behemoth or a neighbourhood pub with a £300,000 turnover, the liability for issues and crisis management remains constant.

In addressing potential issues and crisis risks, every organisation must be prepared to respond to the dynamic landscape of social media, AI-driven digital evolution and the traditional media environment. This readiness encompasses diverse stakeholder groups, both internal and external, and is influenced by economic and political drivers. This change in reputation management caused by AI is another area of increased work in the PR sector.

Developing a comprehensive relationship policy necessitates acknowledging power and volatility intrinsic to internal and external communication and social and AI-driven media as part of the relationship-building mix.

The inherently public (caused by transparency, porosity and agency) nature of these platforms subjects management to extraordinary pressures, underscoring the importance of structured planning and capability maintenance.

In essence, issues and crises can be characterised along four steps towards danger:

Variation: Variations from expected outcomes, financial budgets and timelines are normal aspects of daily management. In social media, this manifests through daily chatter, planned content, anticipated developments, community engagement and supportive commitments.

Foreseen uncertainties: Some variations are identifiable yet unpredictable in their occurrence or timing. While they can be planned for, they are still part of the daily management landscape. Examples include unexpected staff illnesses, which, although unpredictable, are manageable through established mechanisms.

Unforeseen uncertainty: Events in this category are entirely unpredictable during project and risk management planning. There is no contingency plan (Plan B). Crisis management planning is crucial for mitigating the effects of such events. These events may involve dynamic monitoring of conversation, content, volume and focus, quick access to experts and management, scenario planning and "war games" to develop expertise.

Unknown unknowns: these events are particularly nerve-wracking because conventional decision-making tools are inadequate (the COVID pandemic is an example). Developing the capability to manage unknown unknowns is an imperative task for PR practitioners. With a well-trained management team, it becomes possible to identify previously unrecognised risks and alert the organisation and its stakeholders proactively. This enables the organisation to prepare for these unforeseen events that manifest as crises.

While some crises, like the COVID pandemic, fall into the category of unknown unknowns, it is unwise to ignore even the most remote possibilities and not include them into part of the issues and crisis plans with some tools already in place. Such tools will include a hierarchy of responsibility with an escalation process to perhaps fast-track power, the CEO having overall responsibility.

British Defence Intelligence employs a Probability Yardstick infographic to aid in the analysis of issues and crises, demonstrating the organisation's readiness to manage risks.

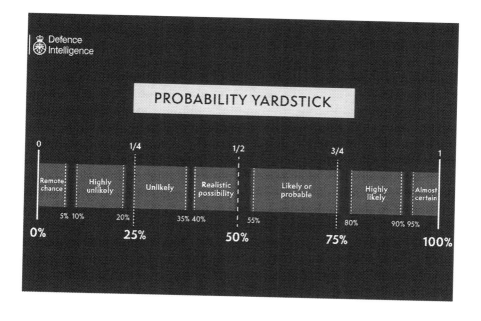

Critical elements of a plan need to be in place early, including:

- A well-versed issues and crisis team for plan development and maintenance.

- Regular and comprehensive audits of the crisis plan.

- Real-time landscaping, monitoring and reporting.

- Integration with broader organisational management, issues and crisis systems.

- Robust internal monitoring and alarm systems.

- Response strategies tailored to various forms of issues and crises.

- Policies and practices for escalation and de-escalation.

STEPS TO TAKE

For the most part, managing issues and crisis (I&C) management is a process.

It begins with acquiring buy-in and authority from the Board to build an issues and crisis plan and assemble an I&C team and a budget (including ROI evaluation see below).

A crisis plan does need a crisis team. They need to be able to come together quickly and make decisions, and implement the plan as soon as a significant issue or crisis is evident.

An I&C plan will ensure that managers can manage issues and identify crises.

The I&C plan must include an ability to understand the wider environment surrounding the organisation and thus be able to see further ahead.

For example, for some organisations, monitoring the national budget and the following public debate may well affect the running costs and employees of the organisation. Having the capability to identify if this will create issues or crises is well worth knowing.

Landscaping reporting and responding must be automated to a considerable degree to keep up with emerging issues and their management.

There are two elements: internal monitoring and external monitoring.

Internal monitoring may well identify days off, days working from home, the number and duration of meetings, attendances, agendas and minutes. It might include numbers and content of emails, phone calls, website access and social media, including frequency, duration and content of pages. Depending on the organisation, the employee's identity might not be used, but then a network of people identified the above internal monitoring will be needed.

For a confidential record, a blockchain can be used (see below).

A time series AI analysis of these data will need to be used to look for variance and escalation/de-escalation of each element.

Because the monitoring is looking for activity tokens (things that happen), running such a monitoring system without identifying personnel is quite possible.

EXTERNAL MONITORING

Monitoring content for tokens that refer to an organisation directly or indirectly is a big project but can be automated.

Just to get some idea of the size of such a project, one can look for a wide range of social media, news sites, websites (Google Alerts is very good at this) and games.

Social-media sites grow well beyond X (Twitter), Facebook, LinkedIn and WhatsApp:

- Facebook
- YouTube
- WhatsApp
- Instagram
- WeChat
- TikTok
- Telegram
- Snapchat
- Kuaishou
- Qzone
- Sina Weibo

- QQ
- X (formerly Twitter)
- Pinterest
- Reddit
- LinkedIn
- Quora
- Discord
- Telegram
- Twitch
- Tumblr

This list is by no means exhaustive, and there are many other social media sites out there, both popular and niche. However, these are some of the world's most widely used social media platforms. Using search engines like Google to monitor content in websites is easy and is available as an API.

It is important to note that some of these social media sites may be more popular in certain countries or regions than others. For example, WeChat is extremely popular in China, but it is not as widely used in other parts of the world.

The elements that might be considered for monitoring are: frequency, media and tracking for significant and unusual change.

There is a lot of software and many good services out there to help. In addition, there are many APIs that can provide very fast and accurate intelligence.

Using (or even creating) AI to monitor such media means that it is possible to track the online actors, what they are saying, who are their 'frends', what subjects do they comment on/create, how many responses do they create/offer and how far do they reach in the close circle and further a wider public and much more.

AI monitoring and time series analysis with analysis of the extent and rate of change across all elements will mean that tracking the reputation, emerging issues and crises can be identified in near real time (or daily or weekly).

Such tracking, analysis and alerting can be for an individual or a nation (why not? The mood of nations towards other nations is very important).

Several AI tools can summarise real-time content, often by scraping the web or using APIs to gather the latest articles, blog posts or other textual information. Some AI tools can accomplish this: News Aggregators with Summary Features: Tools like Feedly, Inoreader and others can aggregate news from multiple sources and offer summary features.

Automated Summary Tools are specifically designed to summarise texts, like SMMRY, SummarizeBot or tools based on OpenAI's GPT models. These can be combined with real-time data feeds to summarise newly published content.

Cloud services like AWS Comprehend or Google's Natural Language API can be used to analyse and summarise large volumes of text.[1]

Using real-time search data to track topics and spot emerging trends with Google's free Trends is another alternative.

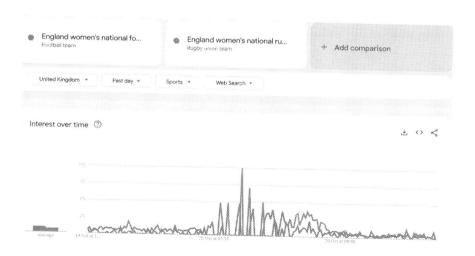

To get summaries of content published in the last hour, one might need to integrate these tools in a workflow that collects the new publications and then applies the summarisation.

Remember always to respect copyright and terms of service when using these tools.

More useful tools can be used to convey content without making it specifically public such as QR codes.

Having interactive software is also very helpful. It can be static of real-time tracking and allows the user to 'see' more because it is graphic.

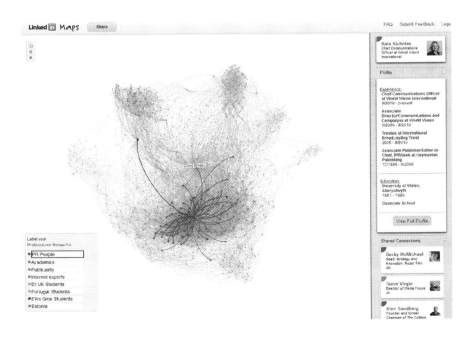

There is a need to create a formal response to issues and crises.

- This will form a formal plan to progressively identify the nature of issues and crises across a range of social media (YouTube, Twitter, etc.) and eventually cover the majority of such media.

- Where an issue of crisis is identified either by automated processes of via escalation through the organisation there has to be a fast means of communication through the issues and crisis management team.

- There is some crossover between media and other operations; these need to be explored and planning developed to optimise monitoring, reporting and response.

- The extent to which issues can be significantly dangerous and mitigation can be developed needs exploring and formal policy developed and implemented.

- The continued evolution of policy and activity needs to be developed to mitigate less helpful public contributions:

- For example the Bank of England faced criticism for its #AskBoE project:
  At first glance, perhaps not so well, given the volume of parody questions ('how long do you think it will [sic] take to destroy the final 1% of Sterling's purchasing power? I have a Prussian friend who is asking'), conspiracy commentary ('What's it like working for a criminal enterprise, stealing ordinary people's money?'), and jabs bank's handling of the global financial crisis ('Why can't I print my own money if I'm insolvent like the Banks too?'). Indeed, the third-most retweeted question, put forward by influential blog @zerohedge, was a sarcastic swipe at the BoE related to its alleged complicity in the foreign exchange rigging scandal in the UK.
  Analysis of these comments and the people posting them offers an opportunity to neutralise them.

This turns criticism into an advantage and should be used as often as possible.

- There is a strong strategic case for organisations to develop alternative forms of communication. For example in the UK, a bank may depend on the BBC/Robert Peston view of events to provide a view of activities. There is a case for developing alternative channels to the broader population using social media AR and VR.

- Equally, there is a cadre of writers in academia and management consultants shaping opinions. Strategic application of social media can offer the means to address their audience without dependence on their outputs.

Sure, here is a summary of the article '7 ways to reduce cybersecurity spend without compromising security' from the World Economic Forum:

- Prioritizing security over convenience. Many organisations cut corners on security in order to save money, but this can often lead to more costly problems down the road. Instead, organisations should focus on implementing the most critical security measures, even if they are more expensive.

- Automating security tasks. There are many security tasks that can be automated, freeing up IT staff to focus on more strategic work. This can help to reduce costs while also improving efficiency.

- Using cloud-based security solutions. Cloud-based security solutions can be more cost-effective than traditional on-premises solutions. They can also be more scalable and easier to manage.

- Investing in security awareness training. Employees are often the weakest link in the security chain. By investing in security awareness training, organisations can help employees to understand the risks and how to protect themselves.

- Partnering with security vendors. Security vendors can provide organisations with a wide range of security solutions and services. By partnering with a reputable vendor, organisations can reduce the cost and complexity of security management.

- Using open-source security tools. There are a number of open-source security tools that can be used to improve security without breaking the bank. These tools can be a valuable resource for organisations of all sizes.

- Benchmarking security spending. By benchmarking their security spending against other organisations, businesses can get a better understanding of whether they are spending too much or too little. This information can be used to make informed decisions about future security investments.

The article also provides some additional tips for reducing cybersecurity spending without compromising security, such as:

- Using security as a service (SaaS). SaaS solutions offer a pay-as-you-go pricing model, which can help to reduce costs.

- Negotiating discounts with security vendors. Many security vendors offer discounts for long-term contracts or bulk purchases.

- Using security best practices. There are many security best practices that can be implemented to improve security without spending a lot of money.

By following these tips, organisations can reduce their cybersecurity spend without compromising security. This can help them to save money and improve their overall security posture.

It is proposed that the organisation identifies a pathfinder group of people to examine this area of risk and crisis management and proposes a structured approach to the development of a social media issues and crisis plan.

There is an element of urgency for this development as organisations get more active and the online community becomes more responsive through social media.

ADDED REFERENCES

When the digital infrastructure is damaged
http://www.techrepublic.com/article/open-data-crowdsourcing-and-sharing-economy-tech-take-on-new-roles-in-disasters/
How Soc med can have corporate or political impact

http://www.wired.com/2014/08/i-liked-everything-i-saw-on-facebook-for-two-days-heres-what-it-did-to-me/

Introduction to the Dark Web and upcoming technologies

http://leverwealth.blogspot.co.uk/2014/08/the-love-at-first-sight-embedded-chip.html?m=1

https://mail.google.com/mail/u/0/?pli=1#inbox/FMfcgzGwHLhfqSFt BZjfbZqnjKhdFVKh

NOTE

1 OpenAI. (2023). *ChatGPT* (September 25 Version) [Large language model]. https://chat.openai.com.

CHAPTER 28

Blockchain

Throughout this book I have referred to blockchain. It is a very useful form of software.

It is important for the reputation of practitioners; it offers an immutable record of activity and can be used to prove the work done by the practitioners.

As we shall see, being able to prove that work has been done and particularly ethically is going to be very important as Artificial Intelligence (AI) becomes ever more pervasive.

Blockchain technology has emerged as a transformative force in today's technological landscape, revolutionising various industries and sectors. Its decentralised and transparent nature provides a robust secure transaction and data management platform. This chapter explores the concept of blockchain and its relevance in public relations (PR) by focussing on its potential role in creating an audit trail for office activities. By leveraging blockchain technology, organisations can enhance their operations' trust, security and transparency.

To comprehend the significance of blockchain technology in PR, it is essential to grasp its underlying principles without delving into technical jargon. Blockchain is a distributed ledger[1] that records information across multiple computers or nodes rather than storing it on a single centralised server. This decentralisation ensures that no single entity has complete control over the network, promoting transparency and eliminating intermediaries.

Key features of blockchain include immutability, wherein once data is recorded on the chain, it cannot be altered or erased; transparency, enabling

DOI: 10.1201/9781003507901-28

all participants to view transactional history; and security through cryptographic[2] algorithms that prevent unauthorised access or tampering.

The implementation of blockchain technology can have profound implications for enhancing trust and security within PR environments. Traditional systems often rely on central authorities for verification purposes. However, this introduces vulnerabilities such as fraud or human error due to contingent reliance.

Organisations can use blockchain as an auditable database system to create an immutable record of work activities through smart contracts (Smart contracts are typically used to automate the execution of an agreement so that all participants can be immediately certain of the outcome, without any intermediary's involvement or time loss. They can also automate a workflow, triggering the next action when predetermined conditions are met)[3] or digital agreements embedded within the chain. This approach eliminates the need for intermediaries while ensuring accuracy in recording critical information.

Using blockchain technology to establish an audit trail offers several advantages over conventional methods employed in office activities. The immutability feature guarantees that once data is recorded on the chain, it cannot be modified without consensus from network participants – ensuring integrity and eliminating the possibility of fraudulent activities.

Additionally, a transparent audit trail provides stakeholders with real-time visibility into work processes. This transparency enhances accountability and facilitates efficient decision-making. As blockchain records transactions chronologically, it creates an accurate historical account that can be referenced when necessary.

Implementing blockchain technology requires careful consideration of technical aspects. Firstly, organisations must determine whether to adopt a public or private blockchain network. Public networks are open to anyone, while private networks restrict access to authorised participants. The choice depends on the desired level of privacy, security and control.

Technical considerations involve selecting the appropriate consensus mechanism (e.g. Proof-of-Work or Proof-of-Stake) and designing smart contracts tailored for specific office activities within PR processes. Additionally, organisations need to address scalability challenges as blockchain technology matures further.

Applying blockchain technology in PR opens up various opportunities for streamlining processes and increasing efficiency. For instance, maintaining a secure database of media contacts through a decentralised system ensures data accuracy while protecting sensitive information from unauthorised access.

Moreover, implementing a blockchain-based audit trail can verify press releases' authenticity by recording the publication date alongside the release itself – preventing subsequent alterations or false claims regarding official statements.

While blockchain presents promising prospects for creating an audit trail in PR activities, several challenges must be addressed. The foremost concern is scalability due to limitations on transaction speed and storage capacity inherent in some existing blockchain platforms. Organisations should carefully evaluate available solutions or invest in exploring new alternatives that can handle higher throughput demands without compromising security or decentralisation.

Another consideration is ensuring regulatory compliance within industries governed by specific guidelines such as GDPR (General Data Protection Regulation). Striking a balance between transparency afforded by public blockchains and privacy requirements necessitates thoughtful implementation strategies to align with legal frameworks effectively.

The future holds immense potential for further advancements in utilising blockchain technology to create an audit trail in office activities, especially within PR. As the technology continues to mature, scalability challenges will soon be overcome through innovative solutions and more powerful and cheaper computing.

Furthermore, integrating blockchain with other emerging technologies, such as artificial intelligence and the Internet of Things, can unlock new possibilities for automation, analytics and data-driven decision-making. Research into these intersections can yield valuable insights that shape the future landscape of PR practices.

Implementing blockchain technology offers significant advantages for creating an audit trail in daily office activities and specifically within PR processes. The inherent features of decentralisation, transparency and immutability contribute to enhancing trustworthiness and, thereby, reputation while also streamlining workflows.

By leveraging blockchain's capabilities effectively, organisations can improve transparency and ensure data integrity and security while simplifying the record-keeping processes. While challenges remain regarding scalability and compliance considerations, continuous research and development will drive innovations that address these hurdles.[4]

It is not necessary to build our own blockchain. There are a number of Software as a Service (SaaS) vendors that can provide such services. Using them, one has to be sure they are available in the long term and data is transferred at some time in the future.

One of the best such services is Ethereum.

Ethereum is a decentralised blockchain platform in the cloud that enables developers to build smart contracts and decentralised applications (dApps). It is known for its versatility, scalability and ability to power complex blockchain-based systems. One of its most significant advantages is creating and managing digital assets, which is a vital aspect of any digital environment.

One of the most exciting applications for Ethereum is the creation of virtual economies. Virtual economies allow users to earn, spend or trade digital assets such as virtual currencies, collectables, Non-Fungible Tokens (NFT) or other unique and rare digital items. Ethereum can power these digital assets by creating smart contracts that can be traded and stored within a decentralised ecosystem, of which more later. As an aside, several developments are attempting to ally smart currencies and other assets to the 'real' world (including the Bank of England's digital pound cryptocurrency initiative[5]).

Another exciting application of Ethereum is the ability to create decentralised autonomous organisations (DAOs). DAOs are organisational structures that use smart contracts to automate decision-making processes without the need for a centralised authority. DAOs could provide a framework for decentralised governance, allowing for more democratic and community-driven decision-making processes.

One apparent challenge is its ability to scale efficiently. Ethereum's current infrastructure, like many other blockchain protocols, has scalability limitations. This limited capacity could slow the development of the Metaverse. However, Ethereum developers are actively working on scaling solutions, such as layer 2 solutions[6] and sharding,[7] that could dramatically increase Ethereum's scalability.

There are a lot of capabilities and programmes available to the practitioner. An example is the integration of M/S Word.

Saving Microsoft Word documents in a blockchain automatically can be done using a third-party service or by developing a custom script.

Several third-party services allow you to save Word documents in a blockchain. These services typically work by converting the Word document to a PDF file and then uploading the PDF to the blockchain. Some popular options include:

- Everledger: Everledger is a blockchain-based platform for tracking the ownership of diamonds and other precious gems. However, it also offers a service for storing and verifying documents, including Word documents.

- DocVerify: DocVerify is a blockchain-based platform for verifying the authenticity of documents. It supports a variety of file formats, including Word documents.

- Proof of Existence: Proof of Existence is a blockchain-based platform for storing and verifying the existence of any type of file. It is a simple and easy-to-use option for saving Word documents to the blockchain.

To use one of these services, you will need to create an account and upload your Word documents. The service will then convert the documents to PDF and upload them to the blockchain. Once your documents are stored in the blockchain, they will be immutable and tamper-proof.

If you are more technical, you can develop a custom script to save Word documents to the blockchain. This approach gives you more control over the process, but it also requires a little more technical expertise.

To develop a custom script, you will need to use a blockchain development platform, such as Ethereum or Hyperledger Fabric. You will also need to create a smart contract that defines the rules for storing and verifying Word documents.

Once you have developed your smart contract, you can write a script that converts Word documents to PDF and then interacts with your smart contract to store the PDFs in the blockchain.

There are a few things to consider when saving Word documents in a blockchain:

- Cost: Saving Word documents in a blockchain can be costly, especially if you are storing a large number of documents. The cost will depend on the specific blockchain platform and service that you use.

- Security: Blockchain platforms are generally very secure, but it is important to use a reputable service and to store your private keys securely.

- Accessibility: Blockchain-stored documents are not as easily accessible as documents stored on a traditional file system. You will need to use a special blockchain browser or wallet to access your documents.

Overall, saving Word documents in a blockchain can be a good way to protect your documents from unauthorised access and modification. However, it is important to consider the cost, security and accessibility of blockchain-based storage before you decide to use this method.

Imagine a club for your chosen sport or hobby, but instead of having a president, treasurer and secretary, all decisions are made together by its members. That's the basic idea behind a Decentralized Autonomous Organisation or DAO.

A DAO is a unique online community where everyone has a say and everything is transparent. Think of it like a club on the blockchain:

- Decentralised: No one person or group controls the DAO, eliminating any hierarchy.

- Autonomous: Rules are encoded in self-executing programs called smart contracts, automatically running the DAO without any human intervention.

- Transparent: All actions and decisions are recorded on a blockchain, permanently available for inspection.

- Community-driven: DAO members propose and vote on proposals, shaping the direction and actions of the organisation.

Now, imagine applying this model to:

- Investment funds: DAO members vote on which projects to invest in, with profits shared amongst everyone.

- Charity: DAOs can collect donations and distribute them transparently to chosen causes.

- Social apps: Imagine a social network where users collectively decide its features and policies.

These are just examples, and the possibilities with DAOs are endless. However, it's important to remember that this technology is still young and faces challenges:

- Technical complexity: Understanding blockchain and smart contracts can be tricky for beginners.
- Legal uncertainty: DAOs exist in a regulatory gray area, posing challenges for legal recognition and compliance.

Despite these challenges, DAOs offer a revolutionary model for democratic and transparent online communities. As a first-year student, you're entering a world where DAOs might shape your future experiences in finance, social interactions and even career choices.

Imagine a vending machine, but instead of selling snacks, it executes agreements between parties automatically. That's essentially what a smart contract is. It's a self-executing contract on a blockchain network, a decentralised and secure digital ledger.

Think of a blockchain as a giant digital spreadsheet that's constantly being updated by multiple computers. Every transaction or interaction that takes place on the blockchain is recorded in this spreadsheet, creating an immutable and transparent record of events.

Smart contracts are like little programs that live on this blockchain. They're written in a specific programming language and contain the terms of an agreement between two or more parties. Once deployed on the blockchain, the smart contract becomes self-executing, meaning it will automatically enforce the terms of the agreement when certain conditions are met.

For example, imagine you want to sell your used textbook to another student. You could create a smart contract that outlines the terms of the sale, such as the price, payment method and delivery details. Once the buyer agrees to the terms, the smart contract will automatically transfer the ownership of the textbook to the buyer and release the payment to the seller.

Smart contracts offer several advantages over traditional contracts:

1. Automation: Smart contracts eliminate the need for intermediaries, such as lawyers or brokers, saving time and money.
2. Security: Smart contracts are stored on the blockchain, making them tamper-proof and resistant to fraud.

3. Transparency: All transactions and interactions on the blockchain are publicly viewable, promoting transparency and trust.

4. Efficiency: Smart contracts can automate complex processes, reducing paperwork and errors.

While smart contracts are still in their early stages of development, they have the potential to revolutionise many industries, including finance, supply chain management, healthcare and even education.

As blockchain technology continues to evolve, smart contracts are poised to play an increasingly important role in shaping the future of society.

Imagine a digital world where ownership is as clear and undeniable as the physical world, where every unique item, from a digital artwork to a virtual trading card, can be verified and traced back to its creator. This is the realm of Non-fungible tokens, or NFTs, the revolutionary technology that's transforming the way we perceive and value digital assets.

Think of NFTs as digital certificates of authenticity, each one embedded with a unique identifier that's immutably recorded on a blockchain, a decentralised ledger that ensures transparency and security. Unlike fungible tokens like Bitcoin, which are interchangeable and indistinguishable, NFTs are irreplaceable, each representing a distinct item with its own intrinsic value.

In the world of art, NFTs have empowered artists to sell their digital creations directly to collectors, cutting out intermediaries and giving them greater control over their work. Musicians can now tokenise their songs, videos and even live performances, creating new avenues for monetisation and fan engagement.

Beyond the realm of creativity, NFTs are poised to revolutionise industries like gaming, where they can be used to represent in-game items, characters and virtual land, giving players true ownership of their digital assets. Even real-world assets like real estate and collectables can be tokenised, paving the way for more efficient and secure transactions.

But the implications of NFTs extend far beyond the virtual sphere. They can potentially transform our understanding of identity, property rights and even governance. Imagine a world where your digital identity is securely anchored to an NFT, providing verifiable proof of your credentials and accomplishments. Or envision a system where property (such as a press release) ownership is transparently recorded on a blockchain, eliminating disputes and streamlining transactions.

The possibilities of NFTs are as vast as the digital realm itself. As technology evolves and adoption grows, NFTs are poised to reshape the way we interact with the digital world, bringing unprecedented levels of ownership, authenticity and value to the virtual landscape.

It is hard to monitor the range of actions that a PR person has to achieve in the daily round.

There is the brief, the proposal, the timetable, the content proposal, research, content drafting, approvals, media listing, distribution, monitoring and evaluation, and responding to client and external effects, and that is just media planning. Then there is strategy management, relations with internal and external stakeholders and issues and crisis management to prepare for. Just identifying, monitoring and updating such activities with reporting on each phase for the purposes of billing and management is a tiresome, costly and time-consuming pain. The room for error is also quite high.

The existing software that manages a PR office's wide range of activities is good. However, it now faces much more significant challenges. The Artificial Intelligence (AI) storm clouds are gathering.

The extent to which AI and AI software-enhanced digital activity will, and to some extent already has, enter the realm of Public Relations is already significant.

Its ability to create capabilities like writing, which can be described as a 'None Tangible Token' and then recast into associated activities, is growing fast and adds a new layer to software already. AI is creating new activities on its own and there is now a need to be able to monitor not just outcomes but inputs as well.

Let's take a simple example. Using AI to recast a case study into a sequence of long and short texts and post for WhatsApp, Twitter and Facebook plus Instagram, the website and LinkedIn together with images and then automatically schedule a sequence of posts is partly available now. A load of the processes happened out of sight. Many are labour-intensive.

But how to monitor such activities and then measure their effects? There is a need to monitor such work and ensure that the activities are recorded in an immutable record.

But blockchain[8] has come to the rescue of the PR industry.

It's early days, but for reasons of efficiency and authenticity, this technology will soon be a big part of PR management because:

1. The data stored cannot be modified. To change it requires a new and different version and block (proof of existence).

2. The data cannot be denied by its owner (non-repudiation).

3. You want decentralisation.

4. You want one source of truth.

5. You want high (immutable) security.

Blockchain technology was initially described in a paper published in 1982[9] and evolved into the digital currency Bitcoin. However, the tech-savvy world soon realised that blockchain could be employed in other ways. Now there are many manifestations of this technology. Where artificial intelligence derives solutions from data, blockchain can ensure the provenance of that data.

With blockchain security, storing information and intellectual assets in the cloud is now possible because it is safe. It's becoming a major factor in the evolving internet.

Mercenne et al. express it thus:

> *Blockchain technology is a significant paradigm shift in software architectures and applications. Indeed, it enables the automation of business workflows, using smart contracts, and hence the collaboration between trusted entities without relying on any centralised or third parties. In this context, the automated generation of smart contracts from high-level business process models has recently received increased interest within the research community.*[10]

NOTES

1 A ledger is a record-keeping system: it tracks value as is moves around, so the viewer can always see exactly what value resides where at a given moment.

2 Cryptographic protocols are sets of procedures and rules that ensure secure communication and provide specific security properties.

3 Smart Contracts are computer programs stored on the blockchain that follow 'if this then that' logic, and are guaranteed to execute according to the rules defined by its code, which cannot be changed once created.

Smart Contacts are automatic, cryptographically secure processes that enable transactions and business functions to happen without trusted intermediaries. Smart contracts on Ethereum put this vision into practice. See https://ethereum.org/en/smart-contracts/.

4 Nicanor Chavez, et al. (2020) 'Securing transparency and governance of organ supply chain through blockchain,' pp. 97–118. doi:10.1007/978-3-030-50613-1_4.

5 https://www.bankofengland.co.uk/the-digital-pound.

6 Layer 2 is built on top of an existing layer 1, like Ethereum, and it aims to increase the capabilities of layer 1. A layer 2 offloads computational work from layer 1 by processing transactions off-chain, increasing transaction speed and throughput.

7 Sharding is a type of database partitioning that separates large databases into smaller, faster more easily managed parts. These smaller parts are called data shards. The word shard means 'a small part of a whole'.

8 Anwar, H. (2023) *The Ultimate Blockchain Technology Guide: A revolution to change the world, 101 Blockchains*. Available at: https://101blockchains.com/ultimate-blockchain-technology-guide/ (Accessed: 02 June 2023).

9 Blockchain was described by Davis Chaum at the University of California at Berkeley (California).

10 Mercenne, L., Brousmiche, K.-L. and Hamida, E.B. (2018) 'Blockchain Studio: A role-based business workflows management system', 2018 IEEE 9th Annual Information Technology, Electronics and Mobile Communication Conference (IEMCON) [Preprint]. doi:10.1109/iemcon.2018.8614879.

CHAPTER 29

Ethics

THE 2023 DOCUMENT 'UNDERSTANDING Artificial Intelligence Ethics and Safety' by The Alan Turing Institute delved into the ethical and safety considerations in the field of artificial intelligence (AI). It aimed to offer a comprehensive overview to serve as a guideline for researchers, practitioners and policymakers. The report identifies key areas of concern, such as fairness, transparency, accountability and safety, providing recommendations and best practices for mitigating risks.

Among its central points is the need for interdisciplinary approaches to address the ethical challenges posed by AI.

It is noteworthy that executives, particularly CEOs, are often considered leaders in shaping AI ethics within organisations. They play a crucial role in setting the tone and direction for ethical AI practices. This trend suggests that CEOs have a significant influence on the ethical considerations surrounding AI technology within their companies.

It is, in light of the changes wrought by the underpinning of AI to civilisation, helpful to examine the nature of corporate ethics.

Corporate ethics refers to the principles and values that guide how a business operates. It encompasses a wide range of issues, including honesty, fairness, responsibility and respect. A strong corporate ethics programme can help businesses to:

- Gain and maintain public trust: When businesses act ethically, they build trust with their customers, employees and the wider community. This trust can lead to better relationships, better employee morale and a stronger reputation.

DOI: 10.1201/9781003507901-29

- Reduce legal risk: Ethical businesses are less likely to be involved in lawsuits or other legal troubles. This can save businesses money and time and protect them from damage to their reputation.

- Make better decisions: Ethical considerations can help businesses to make better decisions that are in the best interests of their stakeholders. This can lead to long-term success and sustainability.

There are a number of different frameworks that businesses can use to develop and implement their corporate ethics programmes. These frameworks typically include elements such as these:

- A code of ethics: A code of ethics is a formal document that outlines the company's values and expectations for employee behaviour.

- Ethics training: Ethics training can help employees understand the company's code of ethics and how to apply it in their daily work.

- Ethics reporting mechanisms: Businesses should have a way for employees to report unethical behaviour without fear of retaliation.

- Ethics audits: Ethics audits can help businesses to identify and address any gaps in their corporate ethics programmes.

Corporate ethics is becoming increasingly important as businesses face growing scrutiny from consumers, regulators and investors. By developing and implementing a strong corporate ethics programme, businesses can gain a competitive advantage and build a more sustainable future.

- In a study by Nielsen, 92% of consumers said they would trust a company more if they were honest and transparent in their communications.

- A study by Edelman found that 74% of consumers said they would boycott a company if they were caught in a lie.

- A study by KPMG found that 75% of CEOs believe that honesty is essential to a company's long-term success.

There is a strong correlation between honesty and sales. Companies that are honest and transparent are more likely to be trusted by consumers, which can lead to increased sales and profits.

Here are some examples of what corporate ethics might look like in practice:

- Code of ethics and conduct: Many companies have a formal code of ethics and conduct that outlines the expected behaviour of employees. This document typically includes integrity, fairness, respect and responsibility guidelines.

- Ethical training and awareness programmes: Corporations often conduct regular training sessions for employees to ensure they are aware of ethical standards and know how to apply them in various situations.

- Transparent and honest communication: Practising open and honest communication with stakeholders, including employees, customers and investors, is a key aspect of corporate ethics. This includes clearly reporting financial performance, business practices and corporate governance.

- Responsible marketing and advertising: Ethical corporations avoid misleading or false advertising and strive to market their products and services responsibly, with respect for consumer rights and dignity.

- Fair labour practices: Ensuring fair labour practices, such as providing a safe working environment, fair wages and respecting employee rights, is a fundamental aspect of corporate ethics.

- Sustainability and environmental responsibility: Many companies now incorporate sustainability into their business models, showing a commitment to environmental stewardship and reducing their ecological footprint.

- Community engagement and philanthropy: Engaging in community service, making charitable donations and supporting social causes reflect a company's commitment to social responsibility.

- Whistleblower protection and anti-retaliation policies: Companies with strong ethical practices protect employees who report unethical or illegal activities, ensuring they are not subject to retaliation.

- Diversity and inclusion: Promoting diversity and ensuring an inclusive work environment where all employees are valued and treated equitably is a sign of ethical corporate culture.

- Compliance with laws and regulations: Adhering to all applicable laws and regulations and going beyond mere compliance to embrace the spirit of these laws are key components of corporate ethics.

- Conflict of interest policies: Establishing clear policies to manage and avoid conflicts of interest helps maintain trust and integrity in business operations.

- Corporate governance: Strong corporate governance, including oversight by a board of directors that is independent and committed to ethical principles, is crucial for maintaining high ethical standards.

Using such examples, a corporate code of ethics can be developed to offer a wider framework. Such a document might run to thousands of words. It can also be offered to employees and other stakeholders as a book (using an AI-supported) self-publishing service – like Amazon). Such a document can also be used to attract new clients for agencies.

A well-developed ethical policy with some examples can then be used to examine, for example, a blockchain of activity that can teach AI to flag up emerging or actual unethical behaviours.

The application of AI could be used to aid in the development of a set of ethical rules or guidelines that would then be used to guide corporate decision-making. The AI can progressively take into account things like corporate values, relevant laws and regulations, and potential impacts on stakeholders. Then, when a decision needs to be made, the AI would provide recommendations based on these ethical rules. This approach is designed to promote consistency and fairness in corporate decision-making and to help avoid ethical lapses.

Andrew Bruce Smith designed an example of this approach at Escherman on ChatGPT+ (https://chat.openai.com/g/g-1cvzvsjWE-cipr-ethical-issue-decision-making-helper).

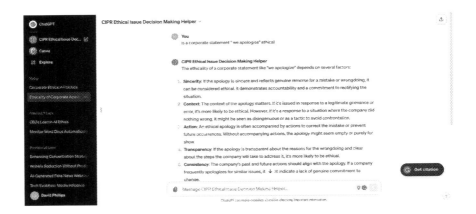

With this example in mind, we discover that AI developments can be applied to aid the application of ethical principles and applied to corporate governance in several ways.

In the future, AI is likely to play an even greater role in corporate governance. As AI systems become more sophisticated and capable, they will be able to help organisations identify and address ethical challenges more comprehensively and effectively.

Here are some specific examples of how AI is already being used to promote ethical corporate governance:

- IBM Watson Ethics: IBM Watson Ethics is a cloud-based platform that helps organisations to identify and mitigate ethical risks in their AI systems. The platform uses AI to analyse large text, code and data datasets to identify potential ethical issues.

- Microsoft Responsible AI Toolkit: The Microsoft Responsible AI Toolkit is a set of tools and resources that help organisations to develop and deploy AI systems responsibly and ethically. The toolkit includes tools to help organisations to assess the fairness, transparency and accountability of their AI systems.

- Google AI Principles: Google AI Principles are a set of ethical principles that guide Google's development and use of AI. The principles include fairness, transparency, accountability and privacy.

Overall, AI is a powerful tool that can be used to promote ethical corporate governance. As AI continues to develop, we expect to see even more innovative and effective ways to use AI to address ethical challenges in the business world.

Ethical considerations do not stop there. Image the ethical issues that surround the use of brain-to-computer communication or the mind-bending application of the metaverse to an immature mind. The application of AI has an ethical element stitched into its very existence.

Such thoughts are well beyond the bounds of this book and need to be developed by institutions such as the Chartered Institute of Public Relations and its academic friends.

AI stands as a potent instrument for promoting ethical corporate governance by enhancing transparency, accountability, and decision-making processes. Through advanced data analytics, AI can detect fraudulent activities, monitor compliance with regulatory standards, and predict potential ethical breaches, thus fostering a culture of integrity within organisations. As AI evolves, it promises even more innovative solutions to ethical challenges in the business realm, such as real-time monitoring of corporate practices and AI-driven ethics advisory systems. However, ethical considerations in AI extend beyond corporate governance. Issues like brain-to-computer communication and the immersive effects of the metaverse highlight the complex ethical landscape surrounding AI technologies. These concerns underscore the necessity for continuous ethical scrutiny and regulation. which institutions like the Chartered Institute of Public Relations (CIPR) and academic bodies must spearhead. Furthermore, technologies like blockchain can augment AI by offering transparent and immutable records of practitioners' behaviors, enabling effective auditing and fostering trust in professional practices. By leveraging AI and blockchain, the efficacy and ethics of professionals in fields such as public relations can be rigorously assessed, thereby enhancing the overall reputation and ethical standards of the profession.

Index

Pages followed by "n" refer to notes.

Printed in the United States
by Baker & Taylor Publisher Services